ECHOES FROM THE VOID

ECHOES FROM THE VOID

Writings on Magic, Visionary Art and the New Consciousness

Nevill Drury

PRISM · UNITY

for Anna, who is my inspiration and my light

Published in Great Britain 1994 by
PRISM PRESS
2 South Street
Bridport
Dorset DT6 3NQ

Distributed in the USA by
THE ATRIUM PUBLISHERS GROUP
PO Box 108
Lower Lake
CA 95457

Published in Australia by
UNITY PRESS
PO Box 532
Woollahra
NSW 2025

ISBN 1 85327 089 X

Typeset by Prism Press, Bridport, Dorset.
Printed by The Guernsey Press Ltd, The Channel Islands.

Echoes From the Void

Spiralling out of shadows, silent
sorcerer rides the night sky
like the laugh of a shooting
star, arching heaven. Gathering
dark chords of beauty, weaving
fragments of mirror, lithe
spirit splinters barriers
of sound and flesh, cracking
open sleep, murmuring
memory into the crevices
of the eye's ear, echoing
infinite
        vaults of
                possibility

Anna Voigt

Contents

Acknowledgements

Several chapters in this book first appeared in 'alternative lifestyle' journals. 'Shamanism and the Earth Mother' was first published in *Simply Living*, while 'Sacred Plants and Mystic Realities — an Interview with Terence McKenna' and 'Computers, Consciousness and Creativity — an Interview with Dr Timothy Leary' first appeared in *Nature and Health*. Permission to reproduce them here is gratefully acknowledged.

'The Supernatural World of Rosaleen Norton' has been published only in Australia (in *Other Temples, Other Gods*: Methuen 1980, now out-of-print), and the reproductions of works by Rosaleen Norton appear courtesy of Wally Glover.

The chapters titled 'The Magic of Austin Spare' and 'Beyond the New Age' have not been published in this form before. 'The Magical Universe', 'Archetypes and Belief Systems', 'The Tarot and Transformation' and 'Surrealism and the Qabalah' were first published in an earlier book, *Inner Visions: Explorations in Magical Consciousness* (Routledge & Kegan Paul, 1979), which for some time has been out-of-print and unavailable.

Introduction

This collection of writings on magic and visionary perspectives contains essays which date back as far as 1972, and consists substantially of independent pieces — several of which have not appeared in book form before. It is certainly representative of my work as a whole and reflects my essential position on the esoteric traditions: that serious occult perspectives should align themselves with the human potential movement and the study of consciousness.

I say this because it seems to me that our society is at a type of spiritual crossroads. Our western culture perpetuates the enshrined belief systems of formal religious institutions but for many people these frameworks no longer bear any relation to the real world. For many, the prevailing orthodoxies have a hollow ring about them and do not reflect deeply felt personal experience. The perspective which emerges with the rise of the human potential movement, however, is one of *spiritual humanism* — the view that all human beings have within them an intrinsic spiritual connection with the Cosmos, an innate potential divinity which can be brought through into conscious fulfilment and recognition. It then becomes a challenge for each of us to explore our own spiritual potentialities and to acknowledge that there are many meaningful pathways to sacred reality.

The Western Esoteric Tradition, which draws variously on High Magic, the mythology of the medieval Tarot, the transformative metaphors of alchemy , the consciousness frameworks of the Qabalah, and the Goddess orientation of Wicca, has contributed substantially to this spiritual humanism — revealing ways of discovering the visionary realms within. However, I feel that for some devotees of magic these approaches have in turn become entrenched, doctrinal belief systems — instead of being seen as exquisite symbolic and metaphorical reflections of the Universal Play of Consciousness. As the noted writer Arthur Machen observed, we need to remember always that all around us is a Cosmos which is essentially mysterious. Any doctrine or method based on the dogma of certainty is bound to be illusory.

On the other hand, if we approach the study of consciousness with a sense of genuine openness I think we discover a lot more. We notice visionaries around us who have tapped into the potentialities of the psyche — who have explored the deeper realms of mind and spirit and experienced both terror and illumination as a consequence. Some of these visionaries are described in this book, and of course there are many more besides. But I feel quite strongly that at this time in our history — a time when many people are expressing feelings of despair, despondency and aimlessness — that we should all seek experiential pathways to the sacred, and learn from each other's individual quests for visionary knowledge.

I also believe that the 'occult' or 'secret' aspects of the Western Esoteric Tradition have well and truly had their day. Occultists should now discard any residual obsessions with grades of hierarchy and elitist notions of ritually structured spiritual attainment. These are really hangovers from the days when western magic was infiltrated by masonic notions of exclusiveness and Victorian concepts of linear progress. Such frameworks are clearly no longer appropriate — the Cosmos doesn't behave that way. Much more important, it seems to me, is the idea of getting worthwhile occult perspectives out in the open — of discovering the many different potentials for visionary expression.

To some extent this collection of essays is a tribute to some of the key thinkers of our era who have pointed the way towards an understanding of spiritual consciousness — figures like Carl Jung, John Lilly and Timothy Leary, among others. But I have also included here a number of visionary eccentrics — like the bohemian trance artists Austin Spare and Rosaleen Norton, and the post-psychedelic radical Terence McKenna. They too have much to offer in the study of magical realities.

We can all learn from each other. I know that I have benefited enormously from my own pursuit of esoteric knowledge and my personal contact with people all over the world who share similar concerns. But the most relevant task now, it seems to me, is to explore the perspectives that can truly transform consciousness. What more rewarding task can there be than the quest for Gnosis ?

Nevill Drury
May 1994

Part One

MAGIC AND COSMOS

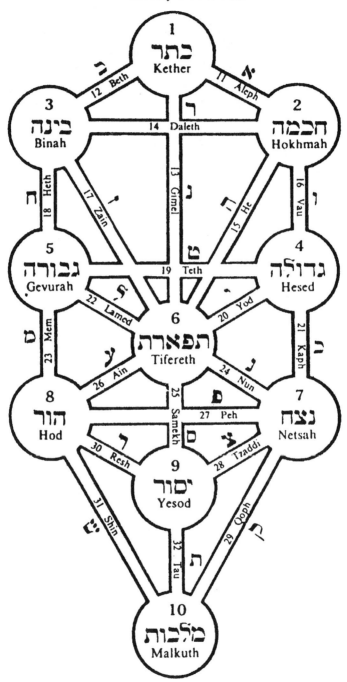

The Tree of Life reveals the pathways to the Godhead

1
The Magical Universe

The English artist and occultist Austin Spare once wrote that the aim of magic was to steal the fire of heaven, and a quite crucial issue is contained in this statement. The magician, unlike the mystic or religious devotee, believes that he has within his scope and potential, the ability to alter his consciousness magically at will — that the gods will respond to him if he undergoes certain ritual activities. It may be that he dresses ceremonially to conjure their energy by capturing their likeness. Perhaps he utters sacred god names like those found in the Qabalah and certain Gnostic formulations, holding to the view that the name actually embodies the essence of the god, and that by uttering the sacred vibration, he is not only tuning into the wavelength of the God-level, but attaining mastery of it.

The idea of will — the sense of being able consciously to bring about a causal effect — is vital to the magical attitude. We find it in the account of Carlos Castaneda, where the magical apprentice has to eat the sacramental drug, whirl the spirit catcher near the sacred water hole and concentrate on the 'spaces' within sounds in order to will the ally to appear.[1] We find it in the magic of Aleister Crowley and the Golden Dawn system in general, where the will enables the magus to rise through the planes of inner space, through the symbolic, mythological energy states of the Tree of Life, and eventually have rapport with the *Higher Self* — anthropomorphized in Crowley's writings as the Holy Guardian Angel.

All of this is quite foreign to most religious systems: prayer and supplication, the offering of thanks to a Saviour god, and ritual activity in a Mass or church service or other worshipful activities, are in no way intended to *capture* the God. Quite the reverse in fact . . . religious devotion is an attitude of mind in which one humbly submits oneself before God in the hope that He will bestow grace and salvation. There is no act of aggression here — no stealing the fire from heaven. One waits, passively, until it is given.

The magical attitude is clearly more active and also more arrogant. The magician is at the centre of his own particular universe. With his sacred formulae, ritual invocations and concentrated will-power, he can bring certain forces to bear. Our first distinction is, then, that the magician believes he can *will* to effect.

The arrogance and even 'primitivism' of this approach has to some extent been made more legitimate by the ascendancy of existential philosophy. It has been common for recent interpreters of the magical tradition to regard the gods of High Magic as emanations and symbols of the creative imagination, forces of the transcendent psyche. Israel Regardie has employed Jungian frameworks of archetypes and energy sources to explain for his contemporary audience what is meant by invoking a God. It is none other than a ritual means of channelling the consciousness into areas described by Jung as the Collective Unconscious, the universal area of the psyche normally inaccessible to man in his everyday activities.

Colin Wilson has similarly related his long involvement with the European existential tradition to a study of modern Western magic, in order to show that such a system of approach offers both a transcendental and an optimistic goal — that man *can* overcome his sensory isolation by in fact gauging more universal modes of consciousness and being.

It is only fair to point out, however, that some occultists view the pantheon of gods as existing in their own right — of being outside the psyche of man — as entities belonging intrinsically to another plane of creation. Magic becomes a means of communication. The gods give knowledge of these esoteric planes to the inquiring magician and allow him to grow in awareness, but they themselves have an identity outside the magician's mind and will. Two examples of magical systems which will be considered, those of the German occultist Franz Bardon, and the Australian witch Rosaleen Norton, both hold this viewpoint.

Magicians, irrespective of their cultural milieu, do tend to share one feature in common and that is the notion of a hierarchy of supernatural beings with whom they interrelate. In fact, remarkably few magical or religious systems are without hierarchy — Zen Buddhism with its 'instant leap into Satori' being a major example.

If contemporary Western magic has had its roots in Gnosticism,

Alchemy, Rosicrucianism and a number of 'pagan' mythologies (the Hellenistic, ancient Egyptian and Celtic systems in particular, all of which exhibit polytheistic features), equivalent hierarchical notions nevertheless present themselves in monotheistic Christianity.

St. Thomas Aquinas and other medieval Christian thinkers proposed a hierarchy of angelic beings which reflected different aspects of God's acts in the world. The Seraphim, Cherubim and Thrones were beings related to God Himself — the Father, Son and Holy Ghost: Dominations, Virtues and Powers related to Universal Creation, and Principalities, Archangels and Angels to individual beings or objects in the world.

Each of these nine orders of Heavenly beings revolved in choirs around God, the Seraphim being closest to God and the Angels furthest removed. The total Heavenly hierarchy thus consisted of God the Father, Son and Holy Ghost, the Virgin Mary, myriads of angels on nine planes, and the order of Saints. [2]

In magic, similarly, the sense of hierarchy is paramount. The medieval *Lesser Key of Solomon* or *Goetia*, which hovers in polarity between black and white magic, contains conjurations to seventy-two devils and also the angels of the hours of day and night, and the signs of the Zodiac. For example, Samael, angelic ruler of the First Hour, is said to have 444 spirits serving under him, and Anael, ruler of the Second Hour has 110. All of this made for most complex and numerous divisions of the supernatural battery of forces encompassing the earth!

Our emphasis in this book is on the modern day, rather than on medieval forms of magical thought, but it is interesting that as recently as 1976, the ceremonial diary of a practitioner of medieval occultism, was published. Georges Chevalier provides in his book *The Sacred Magician* a day-by-day account of his emotional and spiritual reactions in working the lengthy ritual of Abra-Melin the Mage. The actual magical formulation dates from the fifteenth century and takes six months of ritual activity in isolation before the magician is granted communication with his 'Holy Guardian Angel'.

Chevalier's account in many ways is unsatisfactory as a record of magical procedure since it is particularly subjective in style and stresses generalized feelings ('The atmosphere is very difficult around me. Obstacles are being thrown up and I am clumsily stumbling down the path . . .'), rather than a procession of archetypes or magical visions. Chevalier also indicates in his account that he read works such as the Theosophical writings of Alice Bailey and *The Hundred Thousand Songs of Milarepa* during his retreat, thus invalidating to some extent any claim that his results were purely a result of the Abra-Melin method and not produced by meditation on Eastern themes.

However, to attempt a rigorous magical ceremony over such a span of time while remaining in a twentieth century urban context is worthy of note. Interestingly, Chevalier acknowledges a profound sense of spiritual hierarchy. Near the end of his account, at the stage where he has come to identify the regenerative force of his Higher Self, he writes: 'All my communication with the Angels and spirits — with the members of the sub or super-human Hierarchies — is done on [a] high intuitive level . . . .'[3]

Later, having followed the instructions of Abra-Melin which demand that the magician invoke the eight sub-princes and the four spirits of evil, in order to gain mastery over them, Chevalier notes: 'As one progresses along the Path, there are certain "tests and tribulations" . . . a complete trust in God and the Hierarchy will see one through everything.'[4]

One of the most remarkable magical visions of the present century, and certainly the most impressive outside the Golden Dawn tradition, is that of Franz Bardon. Bardon, who died in July 1958 in Germany, was known to his Western occult audience through his writings, rather than as a magical personality as such. He published three major works: *Initiation Into Hermetics, The Practice of Magical Evocation* and *The Key to the True Quabbalah,* of which the second is by far the most significant. In it Bardon outlined a magical universe as detailed and far-reaching as that of the *Lesser Key of Solomon* and *The Sacred Magic of Abra-Melin the Mage.* Even more extraordinary was his claim that his descriptions of the hierarchy of beings on the inner planes were all the result of personal contact!

Bardon's inner world consists of an astral plane girdling the earth which contains the spirits of the four elements, 360 'heads' of the Zodiac (one for each degree of rotation around the planetary sphere), and the 'Intelligences' of the planets radiating upwards from Earth on the cosmic Tree of Life.

Unlike Georges Chevalier, who is extremely humble in his magical encounters (referring to himself time and time again as a worm before God), Bardon takes the more familiar role of the occultist asserting himself on the inner planes. According to Bardon, the magician is the God-Man. He incarnates the Deity, and this places him spiritually above elementals and planetary beings, who are 'incomplete' (a salamander being only a salamander (fire) and a goblin only a goblin (earth) . . .). Consequently all of the hierarchy are obliged to obey him.

Bardon's method is to imagine himself as God, and then evoke a spirit from a particular sphere. However, the magician must know something of the sphere he is entering, for each is a magical domain with its own specific reality. Bardon's claim is that he has worked his way systematically through the astral framework he presents, using as a magical safeguard his own divinity. The occultist in fact wears a crown to symbolize this purity of intent, and also carries a ritual sword to strike fear into the spirits he encounters. Bardon writes: 'From the days of yore, the secret of magic has been restricted to high castes, potentates, kings and high priests . . .' The magician as God is, in a sense, reclaiming inner territory as he ventures from one sphere to another.

The realm of elementals provides Franz Bardon with some of his most complete and detailed descriptions. Below are entries for two supernatural entities, Osipeh, a female elemental of Water, and Ordaphe, a gnome of the Earth:

> *Osipeh* — colour of sign: blue — is a most beautiful water spirit and not only a complete ruler over this element, but also of the magic of water. She likes very much to introduce the magician into the rhythm of the water element by the magic of sounds. She is an excellent singer and dancer as are all her subordinate spirits experts in these arts, and they perform the nicest dances and accompany them with lovely songs. If the magician resists the tempting invitations of this female ruler and gets her under his power, she will place at his disposal several spirits subordinate to her. I know from my own experience that she likes to serve the magician who rules her. . . . [6]

> *Ordaphe* — colour for drawing his sign: black — is a mighty king of gnomes. If the magician so wishes, Ordaphe will lead him through his kingdom and show him all the treasures that are under the earth in the form of ore. He too has a great number of gnomes subordinated to him who do the work designated them under the surface of the earth. Some of them guard the ores, others work on their refinement and maintenance. Ordaphe likes to place gnomes at the disposal of the magician (but) . . . he must never use these spirits for avaricious purposes.'

We recall that mythologically the four elements are personalized into salamanders (fire), sylphs (air), undines, mermaids or mermen (water) and goblins and gnomes (earth). Franz Bardon's symbolic encounters with these entities occur in a trance-like state on a low level of the

astral plane (for the existential magician, the lower reaches of the creative imagination). It is also significant that each entity has a specific
sign or sigil, by which it is summoned. This is coloured appropriately:
Earth = black; Water = blue or silver; Fire = red. (No details are
provided by Bardon for Air, since air elements are said to be 'not at all
pleased with men', and in view of our current ecological problems
with air pollution this is hardly surprising!)

The sigil symbolizes the means of contact and we will encounter
this type of ritualized expression again and again in the magical method.
In the Golden Dawn system the coloured Tattva cards and the elaborate Enochian squares were similarly used as doorways to specific astral spaces. Once again, we find a correlation between the symbol and
the experience of the magician, so that the magical vision, whether of
gnomes, undines or whatever, is directly precipitated by the symbol
of entry. In a similar way, Franz Bardon provides the sigil for each
magical entity as a means of evoking *that one specifically.*

Although Bardon would seem to be implying that the magician has
scaled the full range of creation in taking on the mantle of divine
authority, this is not really the case. The magician is himself evolving,
and for Bardon the process of growth continues as the occultist gains
more and more specific knowledge of each of the inner domains open
to him. He also makes pacts and alliances with high angels and geniuses, who bestow their blessings and talents upon him.

Bardon's magical universe is such that by virtue of his authority he
is free to wander where he will, summoning spirits in the quest for
inner knowledge and then sending them back to their proper sphere
after the encounter. Bardon follows the system of the Qabalah. His
cosmic Tree, which comprises the Zodiac and planetary spheres, grows
upward from the Earth and out of the plane of astral elementals which
has just been described. Bardon, like many other contemporary magicians, is really a shaman. He knows the framework of his inner cosmos, and sees his purpose as venturing on the inner journey up through
its levels of being. Its myriad inhabitants have particular qualities which
identify them. But providing the magician stands in his magical circle,
which symbolizes the divine qualities of the universe, he can come to
no harm:[8]

> The magician who stands in the centre of the magical circle. . . is in fact,
> symbolising the Divine in the Universe . . . furthermore, by standing in
> the centre of the magical circle, the magician also represents the Divine
> in the microcosm and controls and rules these beings in a totalitarian

manner . . . the magician is, at that instant, a perfect magic authority whom all powers and spirits must absolutely obey. . . .

Bardon's method stresses that it is the magician who is in control. Failure to dominate an invoked entity may lead to spirit possession. (Again, in existential terms, this is to allow a forceful mental image to dominate the psychic processes, having wrenched it symbolically out of the creative imagination.)

On the other hand, by assuming the function of divine authority, the magician has open to him all of the spheres and planes of manifestation, together with their varied inhabitants. He is a potential master of them all.

While occultists like Franz Bardon and Georges Chevalier can be fairly stated to have worked outside the occult 'mainstream', the cosmology of the Hermetic Order of the Golden Dawn has had a significant impact on the 'new consciousness' which has emerged as a post-psychedelic phenomenon. Although Eastern systems of thought like *The Tibetan Book of the Dead,* the *I Ching* and certain tracts from the Zen literature captured the imagination of the 1960s counter-culture in its exploration of drug states and peak experiences, it was not long after that the Tarot and Magic became identified as Western equivalents of these mystical philosophies. The influential, though frequently inaccurate, *Morning of the Magicians* of Louis Pauwels and Jacques Bergier, first published in 1960, had already pointed to the existence of the Golden Dawn society as a major esoteric group concerned with charting the potentials of the magical imagination. Later, Aleister Crowley's face showed up alongside Edgar Allan Poe's and many others, on the collage cover of the Beatles' popular psychedelic *Sergeant Peppers* album and the notorious activities of the Manson cult were characteristic of a fascination with occult literature at this time. Anton La Vey, the San Francisco warlock, appeared meanwhile as the Devil in *Rosemary's Baby.*

But there were more wholesome interests too. Arthur Waite's *Rider* Tarot pack has held perennial fascination, and many of his other works, notably *The Holy Kabbalah, The Brotherhood of the Rosy Cross* and his interpretation of the Tarot, which accompanied the pack of cards, were reissued in the 1960s in the United States, as symptomatic of the renewed interest. Israel Regardie's reprinted, edited versions of numerous Crowley works were not far behind.

Since this time, magic has found its way into the lives of pop musicians, psychedelic artists and the suburban populace in general. Sociologists have identified the present occult revival as a predominantly middle-class phenomenon.[9]

It is not surprising that the Golden Dawn model of the magical universe should have had wide-ranging impact for, although it has only recently been subject to thorough historical documentation, the Society first undertook the investigation of the mythological psyche in 1888, and this period in history saw new breakthroughs in the perception of man as a creative being.

Noted psychiatrist, Silvano Arieti, in his recent book *Creativity*, writes that 'it was in 1895 that Freud and Breuer published their book on hysteria which marked the beginning of the psychoanalytic era and opened the road to the study of the unconscious. . . . '[10] He also notes that in the same year Cezanne held his first exhibition of modern 'primitive' paintings which marked a turning away from styles that reproduced Nature, and showed instead a preoccupation with the identity and essence of depicted objects. Visionary modes of art like Cubism and Surrealism followed soon after.

Historically the Golden Dawn followed in the tradition of the European Rosicrucian and Masonic esoteric schools, and the writings of European occultists like Papus and Eliphas Levi were interpreted with interest by Waite and Crowley, the latter claiming Levi as a former incarnation.

But the scope of the Golden Dawn was far broader than that of its predecessors and no occult society since has been able to muster the prodigious range of talent that passed through its ranks: writers of the calibre of W. B. Yeats, scientists like the Astronomer Royal for Scotland, William Peck, and doctors like Wynn Westcott and Edward Berridge. Ithell Colquhoun's *Swords of Wisdom* and Ellic Howe's *Magicians of the Golden Dawn*, which document the society, are perhaps the two most authoritative histories of the Order that have yet been produced.

Our concern here, however, is more with the nature of the magical universe envisaged in the Golden Dawn by its founders and practitioners. More than to any other person the group owes the scope of its magical vision to one man: Samuel Liddell MacGregor Mathers (1854-1918).

It had been common until Mathers's time for occultists and magicians to work single, specific systems. We can turn to Cornelius Agrippa's alchemical treatises, Edward Kelley's skrying in trance and communicating with angels, and Francis Barrett's idiosyncratic magical system, *The Magus, or Celestial Intelligencer* (1801). We find Papus concerned primarily with the origins of Tarot symbolism, Robert Fludd, medieval artist par excellence, infatuated with Rosicrucian imagery, and Thomas Vaughan engaged in a form of tantric alchemy.

Mathers proposed that the Western magician should investigate *all* the cosmologies of his cultural tradition. In 1887 he published the first English translation of Knorr Von Rosenroth's *Kabbala Denudata*, and from it isolated as a major workable framework, the motif of the Tree of Life. His masonic background, and that of his founding colleagues, presupposed an interest in the Egyptian mysteries, which several Masonic authorities claimed as a formative source. Mathers's father was of Scottish descent and, like Yeats, Mathers was fascinated by the Celtic tradition. He was also a member of the pre-Golden Dawn group *Societas Rosicruciana in Anglia* which claimed spiritual connections with Continental Rosicrucianism. The ground of eclecticism was laid. Mathers was a self-taught scholar with a sound knowledge of French, Latin and Greek, and some Coptic and Hebrew. He was later to preoccupy himself in translating a number of key magical documents which might otherwise have been doomed to obscurity in museum archives.

The significance of this wide range of interests was that the magical rituals of the Golden Dawn, in whose shaping and formation Mathers played a major role, came to draw on every major mythology in Western culture.

Consequently what we may term the Golden Dawn cosmology was a very elaborate one indeed, and whereas Franz Bardon's relatively narrow system was based on the Qabalah and a hierarchy of elementals and planetary spirits, Mathers and his colleagues undertook a vast comparative study.

The scope of the magical framework in question is provided by a work entitled *777*, and published by Aleister Crowley as solely his own work. The book is in fact a series of annotated tables of symbols, images and ascriptions which show cross-correlations between religious and magical pantheons, perfumes, minerals, plants and imaginary beings. In his editorial preface to the book, Israel Regardie puts forward the highly unlikely claim that 'Crowley, who had a phenomenal memory, wrote it at Bournemouth in a week without reference books . . .' *777*, at any rate, *was* published privately by Crowley in 1909.[11]

Ithell Colquhoun is of the opinion that Crowley and his friend Allan Bennett, both of whom were disciples of Mathers, borrowed the material, at least in part, from their teacher. She notes that a manuscript entitled *The Book of Correspondences* was circulated among senior Golden Dawn students in the 1890s. There is certainly some thematic evidence in her favour for, if we examine Crowley's Tarot ascriptions as one example, we find that he has opted for what we might call the 'traditional' listing. Readers familiar with his Thoth pack will know that Crowley in fact tampered considerably with the symbolism of these cards — converting the card of Strength into Lust and depicting the Whore of Babylon for example — and in particular he reversed the cards of *The Emperor* and *The Star* in their positions on the Tree of Life. This was in line with his philosophy that 'Every man and woman is a star. . .', which had become a key feature of his magical philosophy since his conversion to Egyptian-based sexual magic in 1904.

Basically *777* uses as its core framework the ten levels of consciousness of the Qabalistic Tree of Life, and the twenty-two interconnecting paths (normally represented by the Major Tarot trumps). Regardie calls the book 'a Qabalistic dictionary of ceremonial magic, oriental mysticism, comparative religion and symbology . . . a handbook for ceremonial invocation and for checking the validity of dreams and visions'.[12] Certainly it is all these things. But from the viewpoint of the purpose of this book I would like to re-state the argument slightly and suggest that *777* represents the parameters of the modern magical imagination.

The construct of the Tree is in itself a cosmological metaphor which describes the hierarchy of energy levels in the manifested universe. The Tree encompasses different states of being from material reality through to infinite inner space. The magician following on its pathways grows in spiritual consciousness as he ascends the Tree, and a variety of methods are open to him. He may meditate on each sphere, rise on the inner planes in trance, or simulate the levels of consciousness imaginatively in ritual. The Tree by itself, as a Jewish mystical symbol, had a monotheistic base however. Mathers and his magical colleagues found that they were able to correlate other mythologies, and polytheistic ones at that, with the levels on the Tree.

The most important correspondences in *777* are thus the tables of deities listed as equivalents in different pantheons. This was an early attempt to cross-correlate archetypes, and the range of comparison was wide indeed. It is here that Regardie may well be right in ascribing certain Oriental sections to Crowley. Crowley travelled widely in the

East and it is likely that the Hindu and Chinese listings were his own work.

When we assemble some of the data of *777* we arrive at something like the following:

Level	Qabalah	Astrology	Egypt	Greek
1.	Kether	Primum Mobile	Harpocrates	Zeus
2	Chokmah	Zodiac/Fixed Stars	Ptah	Uranus
3	Binah	Saturn	Isis	Demeter
4	Chesed	Jupiter	Amoun	Poseidon
5	Geburah	Mars	Horus	Ares
6	Tiphareth	Sol	Ra	Apollo
7	Netzach	Venus	Hathor	Aphrodite
8	Hod	Mercury	Anubis	Hermes
9	Yesod	Luna	Shu	Diana
10	Malkuth	The Elements	Seb	Persephone

Hindu	Precious Stones	Perfumes
Parabrahm	Diamond	Ambergris
Shiva	Star Ruby, Turquoise	Musk
Sakti	Star Sapphire, Pearl	Myrrh, Civet
Indra	Amethyst	Cedar
Varuna, avatar	Ruby	Tobacco
Vishnu-Hari-Krishna-Rama	Topaz	Olibanum
	Emerald	Benzoin, Rose, Sandlewood
Hanuman	Opal	Storax
Ganesha	Quartz	Jasmine
Lakshmi	Rock Crystal	Dittany of Crete

The listings in *777* are of course much more extensive than this and further headings include Scandinavian gods, Buddhist meditations, plants, magical weapons, mineral and vegetable drugs, and the letters of the Greek, Arabic and Coptic alphabets.

The importance of *777* lies in the fact that it was the first attempt in the literature to systematize the various images said to occur at different levels of expanded consciousness. The perfumes and stones listed above were intended as appropriate ritual objects in keeping with the qualities of the invoked god.

When we consider that Freud's initial inroads into the unconscious were in terms of uncovering repressed sexual drives, it is interesting plotting this discovery on the Tree of Life, particularly when we remember that the magicians similarly regarded the Tree as a symbol of the unconscious mind. On the Tree of Man — the archetypal Adam Kadmon is superimposed so that Kether is his crown, Malkuth his feet — we find that Yesod symbolizes the sexual genital region. On a comparative basis, Luna is an appropriate symbol for the monthly cycle in woman and Diana is Queen of the Witches with their fertility worship. Freud's interpretation of the subconscious, by virtue of its dominating sexual emphasis, is thus symbolically based on Yesod. Jung, by comparison delved deeper into the psyche and evolved his theory of individuation — making oneself whole. His emphasis on inner harmony, on the universal symbol of the mandala (or cosmic disc) and on spiritual rebirth, are all appropriate to Tiphareth, the centre of the Tree and 'hub of the wheel'.

Arieti has highlighted Freud's achievement in the 1890s but it is clear that at the same time the magicians of the Golden Dawn were endeavouring to chart parallel mythological processes in the psyche using the method of direct encounter.

777 was compiled gradually and slowly, as the result of visionary explorations of the Order's membership, and by careful examination of the themes in comparative mystical literature. It built very extensively on the important, but simple, correlation suggested by Eliphas Levi of the ten Sephiroth of the Tree and the twenty-two Major Tarot Trumps. As I shall demonstrate subsequently, the Tarot is in itself a profound mythology incorporating all the classical themes of transformation. The framework of the Tree would be bare without it.

There is no question that the above magical correlations have caused anger in certain academic circles. In his most recent work, Gershom Scholem writes: 'The activities of French and English occultists contributed nothing and only served to create considerable confusion between the teachings of the Kabbalah and their own totally unrelated inventions such as the alleged Kabbalistic origin of the Tarot cards . . .'[13]

No informed occultist does of course claim a Kabbalistic *origin* for these cards. What has been suggested, and certainly verified by mystical practice in recent years, is that different religious belief systems overlap in their content. The view in the Golden Dawn was that by correlating common themes in mystical teachings they became more universal in their impact. While the essential individuality of each framework of belief was respected, cross-comparison of the kind undertaken above pointed to the non-exclusiveness of any one school of thought. The belief in the non-exclusiveness of one's beliefs brings with it an attitude of tolerance. By comparison, the political effect of any given heresy is such that, as an alternative belief system, it is often brutally decried on the grounds of its posing a threat to the dominant and therefore 'exclusive' belief systems. The following remarks by Heinrich Zimmer indicate the mythological importance of what was actually a persecuted heretical doctrine in medieval Europe:

> It is my belief that the pictorial script of these [Tarot] face cards represented the degrees of an esoteric order of initiation; employing largely Christian signs, but masking the formulae of the heretical Gnostic teaching that was so widespread in Southern France up to the fifteenth century. The initiate, passing through twenty degrees of gradually amplifying enlightenment and beset by as many characteristic temptations, at last arrived at the stage of a mystical union with the Holy Trinity and this is what was symbolized in the culminating image of the series 'The Dancing Hermaphrodite'. The Soul was the bride of the Lord, the figure of the Hermaphrodite; the two were one. The figure is immediately suggestive of the Dancing Shiva; Shiva unites in himself the Female and the Male. Such a bisexual symbol represents the embodiment in a single form all the pairs of opposites, a transcendence of the contraries of phenomenality; and this incarnate form of forms is then conceived of as the One whose dance is the created world.[14]

Considerable space has been devoted to the Tarot in a subsequent chapter with a view to examining the initiatory themes present in the Tarot symbolism. However, it is apparent that the Golden Dawn method rose above the popular conception of 'magic' and attempted to systematize the same inner realms of the psyche as those investigated by classical psychoanalysis.

There is no doubt that the Golden Dawn system employed trial and error. The ceremonial magicians were required to keep magical diaries of their experiences of encounters with supernatural entities on various of the inner paths. As certain 'constants' emerged, specific deities and images were 'allocated a position on the Tree'. It was at this stage that what began as a quest for archetypes became an affirmation of a particular magical 'programme'. These aspects are discussed in a subsequent comparison of the thought of Carl Jung and John Lilly, for both have relevance to the understanding of the magical process.

The Structure of the Magical Journey

The Tree of Life is the integral framework used in contemporary magic for expanding consciousness. The standard form of interconnecting the ten spheres or *sephiroth* on the Tree is given in the diagram at the beginning of this chapter. This symbol is a visual metaphor which describes the mystical Judaic macrocosm — the process of God becoming real in the world through the process of unfolded creation. As indicated above, with the superimposition of Adam Kadmon upon the Tree, it also comes to represent man's capacity for discovering his spiritual source — *his essential ground of being.*

As Gershom Scholem and other contemporary writers — among them Z'evben Shimon Halevi and Leo Schaya — have shown, the Qabalah is of course a complete system in itself and does not need the Tarot. By the same token, modern ceremonial magic has opted to include it in its eclectic methodology and has similarly experimented with different means of interconnecting the Paths upon the Tree. Traditionally the Tree is the result of an impulse through 'four worlds' — *Atziluth*: Principles; *Briah*: Creativity; *Yetzirah:* Formative Imagination and *Assiah:* Activities. The four worlds straddle ten levels of being and these can be listed briefly as follows: Atziluth is the world of archetypes, the very essence of creation. Beneath this plane, in Briah, these archetypes begin to crystallize into specific ideas, and in Yetzirah definite forms appear whose familiar counterparts may be found in the archetypal images of the unconscious mind. In the fourth world, Assiah, the manifesting forms of creation finally become real in the sense we know them normally.

The ten spheres of the Tree of Life embrace these four worlds, and man, as the microcosm, thus has a spiritual counterpart at all of these levels. The magician actively seeks knowledge of these inner states and the Tree and its associated paths of the Tarot constitute a framework for exploring transcendental states of consciousness.

2

Archetypes and Belief Systems — the Relevance of C. G. Jung and John Lilly

It is hardly surprising that in endeavouring to explain magical frameworks psychologically, most contemporary occultists have indicated a preference for the analysis of C. G. Jung. In Jung's writings we discover a remarkably rich synthesis in his treatment of mythology and legend and its relation to the primordial imagery of the psyche. While Jung was probably unaware of the existence of the Golden Dawn, he nevertheless notes that the 'image series of the Tarot cards were descendants of the archetypes of transformation',[1] and he provides, with his conceptual divisions of the psyche into the personal and collective unconscious, an important basis for understanding the workings of the magical imagination.

In Israel Regardie's view man has discovered that 'a barrier of inhibition is built up between the unconscious and conscious thinking self . . . we have become cut off from our roots, and have no power, no ability to contact the deeper, the instinctual, the most potent side of our natures'.[2] For him, the symbolism of magic — with its meditative and ceremonial aids acting as catalysts to the imagination — provides a means of breaking down this barrier. The magician comes to realize this identity and unite with the unconscious self.

I have referred earlier to the shamanistic exploration upon the Tree of Life and also to the related out-of-the-body/trance state which accompanies it. Regardie, like most occultists, identifies the so-called astral planes, the inner mythological domain, with Jung's concept of the collective unconscious.

In *The Structure of the Psyche* Jung claimed that the collective unconscious 'contains the whole spiritual heritage of mankind's evolution born anew in the brain structure of every individual'.[3] Its dominant primordial images he called 'archetypes' — identifying them as the deepest and most profound strata of the mind.

The influential English occultist W. E. Butler, who trained under Dion Fortune in the Fraternity of the Inner Light, commented on the parallels between the Collective Unconscious and the magician's cosmological territory: 'Magic, with its roots in the immemorial past . . . speaks to the subconscious mind of man through the archaic images of its symbols and rituals and thereby provides those "changes in consciousness" which the magician seeks.'[4] Butler is here referring to Dion Fortune's definition of magic as the technique of changing one's consciousness subject to will. The magical aim is to explore and integrate the universal imagery of the psyche which is symbolic of the higher self.

Jung regarded the Collective Unconscious as 'objective' — it was able to resist the artificial ordering processes conceived by the personal consciousness. And yet the 'universal' domain has for many remained unacknowledged as a source of inner stability.

As contemporary writers like Theodore Roszak and Stephen Larsen have noted, modern man — with his hankering for gurus and spiritual therapy — seems to be expressing a need to reaffirm his contact with these 'sacred' realms of being. If the present occult revival is a symptom of this need, it is understandable that the Golden Dawn system of magic and Jung's formulation of the mythological unconscious should embrace similar territory.

Jolande Jacobi, in a concise exposition of Jung's views on archetypes writes:

> In every single individual psyche they can awaken to new life, exert their magic power and condense into a kind of 'individual mythology' which presents an impressive parallel to the great traditional mythologies of all peoples and epochs, concretizing as it were, their origin, essence and meaning and throwing new light on them . . . The archetype as the primal source of all human experience lies in the unconscious, whence it reaches into our lives. Thus it becomes imperative to resolve its projections, to raise its contents to consciousness.[5]

MacGregor Mathers and his colleagues in the Golden Dawn were quick to perceive the implications of the Tarot and Qabalah as a means for plumbing these normally unconscious depths. Their ritual activity was specifically orientated initially to awakening in each of the Golden Dawn members an awareness of the four lowest mythological *sephiroth* on the Tree of Life. This was followed — at the more advanced stages of initiation in the so-called Second Order — by the ceremony culminating in the attainment of Tiphareth or rebirth consciousness. Tiphareth may be regarded as the centre of a mandala delineated upon the Qabalistic Tree. As a state of consciousness associated with spiritual rebirth, the magician awakens in his own consciousness the sense of the God-man. Tiphareth is a symbol both of transformation and individuation. it is a transformatory experience in the sense that it leads higher up the Middle Pillar to universal consciousness — the state devoid of all notions of individuality — but it is also an important stage in individuation as the centre of the mandala of inner man. As Edward Edinger has said, 'individuation is a process not a realised goal. Each new level of integration must submit to further transformation . . .'⁶ The shaman does not rest in Tiphareth — he pushes on further up the Tree.

It is this sense of spiritual evolution — expressed in Jung's work as the search for inner wholeness — which again characteristically links his psychological model to that of modern magic.

According to Butler, 'It is here that the fourth instinct (i.e. the Religious Instinct) posited by Jung comes in, for it is the counterpole drawing the developing man up to greater heights and we might with advantage equate this fourth drive with what the occultists call the Superconscious or Higher Self.'⁷ Dion Fortune similarly regarded 'the Microcosmic Archetypes — such as the Father, Mother, Magician and Wise Woman (as representing) the linking of the developing soul with certain 'lines of force' in the macrocosm, or in other words, the bringing of the manhood to God or the Gods.'⁸ She followed Jung in characterizing these archetypes as 'objective' — as intrinsic symbolic vortexes in the psyche, representative of 'creative evolution'.

A study of the Tarot, especially, reveals a mix of all of Jung's dominant archetypes. As aspects of the Great Father we find *The Emperor, The Hierophant* and *The Charioteer,* while the Great Mother is represented by *The Empress, Justice* and as Mother Nature subduing the Lion of *Strength.* The Divine Child is found expressed in both polarities with the dancing children of *The Sun* and *The Lovers.* The Divine Maiden is depicted on *The Star, The World* and *The High Priestess,* just as the Trickster — whom Jung describes as 'the forerunner of the saviour, and like him God, man and animal at once' — is superbly portrayed in the form of *The Devil.* A master of delusion, the Devil, with his sagging breast and hairy torso is a mockery of the Divine Hermaphrodite. The archetype of the Wise Old Man 'who penetrates the chaotic darkness of mere life with the light of meaning' is shown in the form of *The Hermit* who treads towards the Void holding his shining lantern.

Jung refers to symbols as 'transformers of energy'[9] and he distinguishes symbols from signs, which are dead, secular representations without any connotation of mystery.

The meditative trance method of the Tattvas, the Enochian squares and the Tarot which will be discussed subsequently, is such that the magician chooses a path of entry which precipitates a specific mythological process — a visionary encounter with the Gods upon the Tree. The inner symbolic domain entered by this means is undoubtedly directly related to the nature of the symbolic doorway. As such these cards take on the same function as a mandala — they are what Jung calls 'a centering effect' for concentration — 'they not only express order, they also bring it about.'[10] The entire notion of *magical order and control* — of choosing a specific Tarot card, of invoking god-names for protection, of remaining within the magical circle (another mandala symbol) and of banishing chaos (evil) as a prelude to ceremonial — such controls are designed to integrate all of the magician's psychic experiences into his consciousness, subject to his will.

Jolande Jacobi notes that any such union, whether through ritual enactment or by shamanistic trance, with archetypal sources, constitutes an evolutionary expansion of consciousness. 'If once the transformed individual has recognized himself as "God's image and likeness" in the deepest sense, the sense of ethical obligation, he will, as Jung says, become "on one side a being of superior wisdom, on the other a being of superior will".'[11]

It may be appropriate to retrace, in the Jungian sense, the archetypal domain of the contemporary magician. At the core of the magical cosmology we find a four-fold division of archetypes into FATHER-MOTHER-SON-DAUGHTER which is often said to be based on the four-fold sacred name of God, JHVH. Within the monotheistic framework of the Tree of Life it becomes possible to correlate other mythologies. The two most complete pantheons, which provided the dominant inspiration for ceremonial magic and meditative purposes in the Golden Dawn, were the Egyptian and the Graeco-Roman. The creation process in the Qabalah is regarded as one of gradual development, while in ancient Greece with the interrelations of so many of the gods the process was necessarily less linear. And whereas on the Tree itself the level of 'earth consciousness' is the *end-result* of the cosmic process, in Egyptian mythology the creation occurs as a result of the separation of the earth and the sky. Consequently, although there are correlations of archetypes they do not always arise in the same sequence in their respective mythologies.

The magical cosmology of the Tree of Life is as follows:

KETHER-The first manifestation of creation from the Infinity of non-existence beyond. Transcendent above the duality of good and evil, male and female or force and form, this profound state of cosmic consciousness is symbolized mythologically by the Divine Hermaphrodite.

CHOKMAH and BINAH — As the great impulses of force and form these emanations are symbolized by the Great Father, who provides the spark or sperm of creative manifestation, and the Great Mother who is the womb of the World. Their cosmic marriage is a sacred mystery, however, for as a conjunction they complete the Trinity and remain beyond the actual workings of the created universe itself.

The remaining *sephiroth* are the Seven Days of Creation headed by a 'lower' (or more manifest) aspect of the Father archetype who acts as guardian of the world.

In CHESED and CEBURAH he shows his two dynamic aspects of Mercy and Severity, revealing the universe to be an ongoing process of life, destruction and renewal.

TIPHARETH is the consciousness level of the God-man — the divine Son who mythologically encompasses the Sun and the process of spiritual rebirth.

NETZACH is one of three subsequent emanations which reflect in mythological terms lesser aspects of the Great Mother and in turn are linked to the Moon. Netzach represents emotional love and equates with the love of the divine Son for the world.

The other feminine levels of consciousness are the ninth and tenth sephiroth YESOD and MALKUTH which come to represent the sexual instincts and the fertile earth itself.

HOD, the eighth sephirah, like Tiphareth, is a 'lower' masculine form -and bears a strong relation to Chokmah. Its deities are often messengers of the gods — intermediaries between transcendence and physical reality.

In the sense that the shaman or magician is entering the inner domain at the level of earth consciousness in order to proceed to the more transcendental states, the sequence is now reversed.

First level

MALKUTH Associated with crops, the harvest and the living environment, this sphere is closely related to gods of vegetation, especially
in their seasonal, cyclic aspects. In Egyptian mythology the representative deity was Geb, with mountains and valleys forming the un-
dulations of his body. In Greece the myth of Persephone went beyond the representation of the actual world in relating the life-death
polarity of the wheat grain cycle. Snatched into the underworld by
Hades/Aidoneus, Persephone later spent the winter months in his
realm as the fearsome queen of death and the other six months on
earth with Demeter, goddess of the abundant harvest. Persephone thus
symbolizes the growth and decay of the cereal crop itself.

YESOD is the seat of the sexual instinct, called Nephesch in the
Qabalah and linked to lunar myths of fertility. In Egypt, Isis is the
wife of the solar deity Osiris and is a great magical enchantress and
healer. She recreates the phallus of the slain Osiris and gives birth to
Horus by him. The Greek lunar deity meanwhile had three faces — as
Selene (the Moon), as Artemis (goddess of the witches and guardian of
herbal, medicinal secrets) and as Hecate, who as scourge of the underworld was sometimes combined with the dark face of Persephone.

HOD equates with intellect, rational thought and order, and
mythologically has come to be linked with Thoth and Hermes who
were themselves combined as deities during the Greek period in ancient Egypt. Thoth is the inventor of speech, the divine intelligence, a
great magician and the scribe and representative of the gods. He also
has some connections with the Moon — which is mythologically dominant as a symbol on this part of the Tree. Thoth in his aspect of inter-
relating with the world may be ascribed to Hod, as can Anubis the
jackal god of death. Anubis was the offspring of Osiris, the Sun god
(the moon similarly reflecting the Sun as a child reflects it parent).
Hermes also had connections with the dead, one of his tasks being to
conduct the deceased souls to Hades.

On the Tarot card *Judgment* which joins Malkuth and Hod and
which forms a triangular aspect with Yesod, we are shown human
beings rising forth from their tombs to the note of a heraldic trumpet.
Mantric sound and transition through death — which itself is symbolic of the lower unconscious mind — are notable features both of

Hod and the lower mythological domain upon the Tree.

NETZACH, with its focus on love and emotions, counterbalances the less subjective and more orderly forms associated with Hod. In Egyptian mythology Isis once again — as the lover and wife of Osiris — and Hathor with her symbol of the solar disc, are female counterparts of the solar god. Nephthys, the wife of Osiris' tyrannous brother Set, presents with her husband the dark face of these two archetypes and both reflect to some extent Jung's concept of the 'trickster' archetype. Aphrodite as the Greek goddess of love and beauty, was said to have been born in the ocean foam near the island of Cythera. But just as Netzach is a development from the sexual regions of Yesod, so too is Aphrodite a sensuous lover. She has numerous amours with Ares, Hermes, Dionysus, Anchises and others. She is also representative of the reproductive powers in Nature and as such is a lower form of the Great Mother — the Womb of the Universe.

TIPHARETH is the centre of the Tree, the solar vortex in inner man — the mediating stage between man and godhead on the mystical ascent. A sphere of beauty, life and harmony, Tiphareth is associated with deities of life and light, rebirth and resurrection. It is also the sphere of sacrifice, for the more limited terrestrial personality is now offered by the shaman in place of universal understanding and insight. In Egyptian cosmology the resurrected Osiris, the Sun-god who rules triumphantly over the forms of darkness in the underworld Halls of Judgment, profoundly demonstrates the triumph of renewal. The Greek Helios-Apollo was similarly god of the Sun, healer and destroyer of monsters (the negative forms of existence). He and Artemis are twin brother and sister (sun and moon), just as Geb and Nu (earth and sky) gave rise to Osiris and Isis (sun and moon) in Egyptian cosmology.

GEBURAH is the archetype of the warrior or the wrathful face of the Great Father, Horus, as avenger of his father Osiris' death, became the model for the pharaoh kings. We find his medieval equivalent in *The Charioteer* of the major Tarot arcana. In Greece Ares was god of war, champion of Troy and the lover of Aphrodite. Interestingly, on the Tree of Life Geburah and Netzach form a diagonal balance with one another. There are also elements of an angry Poseidon in *The Charioteer* for he drives his chariot vengefully through the ocean of form — destroying outmoded creation in order to make way for new impulses of life.

CHESED parallels GEBURAH but presents a more passive watchful aspect. Ra, in the Egyptian system, was father of the gods and mankind — not himself the creator of the universe, but its maintainer. Zeus plays a similar role. While he is not the originator of the world we see him as the most powerful of the gods and respected, despite his numerous procreative activities outside his marriage to Hera, as the embodiment of justice.

Beyond these archetypal areas we begin to move into the domain regarded as the Primal Mystery. The Great Mother and Father are still present as symbolic images although the symbol itself has less relevance in this transcendental region.

BINAH AND CHOKMAH The marriage of Shu (the atmosphere) with Tefnut (life principle) produced the more 'regional' or 'terrestrial' Egyptian deities Osiris and Isis.

Similarly, while Zeus was thought to dominate actual creation, he was himself the son of Cronus and Rhea. Cronus was one of the Titans and Rhea was the 'Great Mother of the Gods'. On the Tree of Life the most exalted stage of consciousness, the Monad, is KETHER — the Crown. Frequently the symbolic image of Kether is hermaphroditic — in alchemy the king and queen wedded into a single body. In the Gnosticism of Basilides the creator god Abraxas contained the polarities of both good and evil.

The cosmology of Heliopolis regarded Atum the creator as being originally bisexual. He later came to be identified with Ra and was symbolized by the Bennu bird or phoenix, a lower-order solar symbol.

In Memphis the creator was Ptah and in Thebes Amon, but invariably the creator was believed to emerge from the infinite space of Nu. In Greek mythology the comparable deity was Ouranos — Father Sky, the most ancient of all the gods who, with Gaea, gave rise to the archetypal parents Cronus and Rhea.

It is clear that these profound mythologies eventually taper off into an ineffable mystery. The consciousness states which these deities represent are part of a system of belief which is open-ended or limitless. In fact the structure of these accumulated mythologies is potentially so vast that it embraces the entire range of inspirational levels, not only of the Western magical imagination, but also of the creative psyche itself.

In so far as any magician seeks to rediscover the actual sources of creative activity he is likely to apply some system of activating these archetypes. Unfortunately the occult tradition has frequently clouded its aims in power struggles and other non-mythological activities. A study of modern occult sources shows all the revealing signs of dogma and literalism which have been decried vigorously as faults in other religious institutions. [12]

All too often magical devotees have been asked to believe in 'adepts and secret chiefs', 'root races', 'angelic and demonic beings', astral vibrations and ritual formulae, without any meaningful explanation of what is really meant by these concepts.

In view of these tendencies towards dogma it is interesting to note the views of John Lilly who has produced a perceptive exposition, in *Simulations of God*, of the nature of belief itself.

A given archetype — as an image of illumination — may manifest itself in a variety of cultural practices and religious beliefs. If the practitioners of a belief system are sufficiently convinced of the exclusiveness of their own particular expression they may be given to religious crusades, conflicts with rival factions, or other extremist behaviour. Alternatively they may acquire excessive pride and 'devotional smugness' and endeavour to clasp to themselves their secret and sacred truths. One of John Lilly's main avenues of inquiry has been to consider the effect beliefs have on those who adhere to them.

In *Simulations of God* he writes: [13]

> Dogma arises when one asserts the exclusiveness and 'truth' of a specific belief system. Mystical experiences can be used to support dogma ... to extend into proofs of belief systems. All we are calling to attention here is that if one forms the basic belief that these phenomena originate from a God Out There, from the results of one's use of rituals directed to a God Out There and from a prayer to a God Out There, then one is not exploring all the possibilities . . .

Lilly raises the important issue that the belief system can act as a constraint upon any insights, intuition or illumination which may arise. In one sense The Tree of Life system *is* an imposition; it becomes less so if we realize its metaphorical symbolic qualities and the essentially mysterious states of being which it delineates.

John Lilly's investigation of belief systems dates from his well-known explorations of transcendental states by means of a sensory-deprivation tank. He investigated the idea that as one's external sources of stimulation are closed off, the mind manifests certain belief patterns which have already been programmed by 'the human biocomputer'.

His initial work consisted in charting certain inner spaces — in particular those investigated by Oscar Ichazo and Gurdjieff and detailed in the Arica training, and more recently the Zen states of Franklin Merrell Wolff. His views on the relativity of systems of belief are particularly relevant to the study of magic since for some the symbol of the Tree of Life has acquired the status of an intrinsic attribute of the mind.

Lilly points out that what we are all dealing with is a system of metaphors. The more impressive metaphors span a wide spectrum of consciousness, while the less impressive ones are restrictive: mind containing, rather than mind-revealing.

Mircea Eliade has suggested that the Western mind has a tendency towards 'linear' forms and tends to conceptualize in terms of beginnings and endings whereas the Eastern psyche gives more status to infinite cycles.[14] If Eliade is right, and the Tree of Life (for all its poetic beauty) is superficially a mesh of points which define and structure, we are perhaps wise to remember its *intangible* qualities: the Tree is a *metaphor* for imposing order on the chaos of the unconscious. It is ultimately *open-ended* since Kether expands into the infinite Light and Space of Ain Soph Aur. The modern magical Qabalah is itself a system of manipulating symbols but then *casting them into the Void* once their reality is transcended — as seen with the Tarot. *The Fool* is depicted throwing away his possessions and dancing into a chasm of Non-Being.

Lilly writes:

> To remain open-ended one's God must be huge — in order to include one's ignorance, the unknown, the ineffable. Instead of God as the Belief, the Simulation, the Model, one adheres to God as Mystery, God as the Unknown. The explorer of the inner spaces cannot afford the baggage of fixed beliefs. This baggage is too heavy, too limited and too limiting to allow further exploration.[15]

In the contemporary context the shamanistic magician venturing in the astral domains of the Tree retains a vigilant alertness while not wishing to limit his symbolic ingress. He may meet illuminating or terrifying magical creatures, he may travel through exciting and exotic landscapes or murky elastic limbo states, but it is his belief system — the extent to which he ascribes reality to particular symbolic forms — which will contain him. One imagines as an extreme example, the psychic wanderings of a devout fundamentalist Roman Catholic fearful of the negative side of his belief system — the infinite and immensely painful torment of hell flames licking his flesh. In the sense of John Lilly's explanation he stands trapped by the limit of his belief. Our same devotee automatically passes through the flame imagery when he ascribes non-reality to it, thus making his doctrinal belief open-ended. In the same way, we are reminded of the Avam Samoyed shaman who travels in trance to the domain of the cosmic blacksmith, working a bellows over a huge fire in the bowels of the earth. The shaman is slain and boiled over the fire in a cauldron for 'three years'. The blacksmith then forges him a new head, instructs him in mystical powers and reconstitutes his body. The shaman awakes as a revivified being. [16]

Considered as a perceptual reality in the fantasy realm of trance such a shaman would endure intolerable mental agony if he identified with the dismembering process. Seen, however, as a rite of transformation in which the shaman dispassionately observes his own rebirth initiation, the process acquires a quite different significance and magical effect. Dismemberment and rebirth are common themes in world mythology. *Death* complements *The Devil* as a predecessor to rebirth in the Tarot arcana and its symbolic content parallels that of our Samoyed shaman. *Death* depicts an angry skeleton wielding a scythe through a crop of human heads. But on closer examination we discover that the skeleton symbolizes the death of negative human limitations — he is hacking away the empty shell of the 'persona'. The 'essence' of each apparently dismembered being flows onwards in the sanctified stream of life towards the inner sun of Tiphareth.

Seen as an end in itself — a ghastly inner hell of wanton destruction — the symbolic location of *Death* is indeed horrific. Viewed as a path of transformation it takes a different perspective. The shaman does not impose a limit to his magical perception and, instead of identifying with the incarcerated body, flows with the stream into a different — and in this case revivifying — domain.

It is the act of symbolic re-emergence, the re-fortification of the shaman himself, which makes him a new man. In psychological terms he has come through his rite of passage as an integrated personality rather than as a schizophrenic. Silvano Arieti, writing on the distinction to be drawn between schizophrenics and mystics, notes:

> The hallucinatory and delusional experiences of the schizophrenic are generally accompanied by a more or less apparent disintegration of the whole person. Religious and mystical experiences seem instead to result

in a strengthening and enriching of the personality.[17]

Accordingly, the shaman's role is one of emerging whole. In Jung's terminology this is the core of the individuation process; within Lilly's framework the mystical programme is effective because it takes the shaman into a space where he overcomes his limit — his terrestrial personality — and is reborn into the cosmos.

The programme and the means of entry
While Lilly has acknowledged his indebtedness to Jung, there is an important distinction of emphasis between them. In Jung's work the archetypes are intrinsic; they are profound universal images imbedded in the psyche of man irrespective of his cultural determinants. The latter merely clothe each archetype with an outer form intelligible to the culture concerned, and manifest accordingly in religious and mystical beliefs. It was the parallel idea that world mythologies correlate which gave rise in the Golden Dawn to the creation of the tables of reference found in *777*.

With Lilly, intrinsic constants, or universals *per se,* are not the key factor. What is more important is the range of consciousness made possible by a set of symbols. He asks: 'What are the *limits* of belief — then these are limits to be transcended.' Characteristically in his studies he has chosen especially open-ended cosmologies as his basis — the Zen system in particular. In Lilly's view it is not so important to indicate the existence of specific archetypes, such as the God-man, as to ensure that they are part of the programme adopted for the venture into the inner domain. Without symbols of transformation, for example, a programme for inner space would be especially barren.

In this sense the endeavour in *777* to correlate, for example, the hexagrams of the *I Ching* with the Qabalah and the Tarot and a myriad of other symbols, misses the point. While it is valuable to be aware of correlating mythologies, each set of symbols is distinctive to itself. Each taken as a pathway may cover comparable territory, but in the long run the shaman must choose one language of symbolism in which to converse or else his communication becomes gibberish. To attempt to conglomerate elements of the *I Ching,* Tarot and Norse mythology as parallel processes has the potential effect of introducing chaos into the programme and disrupts each system's unique expression of the universal process.

Lilly's direction is, it would seem, long overdue in the domain of occult practice. The Western magical tradition is extraordinarily diverse, embracing as it does elements as far reaching as the *notarikon* and *gematria* in the Qabalah, coagulation and distillation in spiritual alchemy, the cosmology of Christian Rosencreutz and the medieval symbolism of the Tarot. Lilly asks us by implication to make a choice: — if these magical elements do embrace the same inner terrain of the psyche, why clutter the programme? Why feed repetitive symbolic data into the human biocomputer? Why attempt to assimilate a vast mass of esoteric lore, from the intricacies of Enochian grammar through to the 72-letter sacred name of God, when in fact all we are after is the state of consciousness which takes us through the process of rebirth and 'emergence'?

I have indicated earlier that modern magical procedure, in effect, programmes the imagination. An earth Tattva symbol produces visions of earth — in all likelihood involving anthropomorphic goblin forms such as are described in the writings of Franz Bardon.

In *The Dyadic Cyclone,* John Lilly describes the effects of consciously working within a state of coma produced by a fall in a bicycle accident. Lilly found himself able to focus meditatively in this comatose condition and used as an entry symbol the inverted ר motif found in Spencer Brown's mathematical treatise *The Laws of Form.* This symbol in mathematical terms symbolizes a type of stress point between containment (the inner area of the symbol) and non-containment (the area beyond it) which Lilly refers to as the 'marked' and 'unmarked' states. As with the magical paths of entry, Lilly found himself in trance entering a space linked to his focusing symbol.

The marked state induced a perceptual experience of a specific planet in space where catastrophic, self-destructive wars were occurring — emblematic of a limited, non-organic point of view. The unmarked state produced by his dualistic symbol gave rise, on the other hand, to an experience of the Void — 'of vast inner SPACE'. He found himself travelling as if at sub-atomic levels from one universe to another in regions where 'space itself is indeterminate'. By its very nature Lilly's focusing sigil ר was able to produce each of these polar possibilities.[18]

In comparing the approaches of Jung and Lilly and their relevance to understanding the magical imagination it is clear that a different sense of value may be ascribed to each. Jung indicates the depth and universality of the primordial imagery which is the terrain of the shaman's venture inwards. Lilly, on the other hand, lays emphasis on the range of consciousness offered by any set of symbols and provides in turn the essence of a technique. Once the shaman is assured that his chosen path embraces archetypes of transformation, his programme of entry can be as simple and as clear-minded as required. As a study of the Tarot shows, Tiphareth as a rebirth state may be reached by passage through just two symbolic inner spaces — represented by *The World* and *Temperance*. The role of the magician is to endeavour to build up his perception of the alternative reality presented by these symbols and, then, transcend them. In Lilly's work we find an important implication — that it is not necessary to programme esoteric complexity into the human biocomputer. We also have the option of 'authentic' simplicity.

3
The Tarot and Transformation

All shamans, whether in Siberia, Indonesia or Middle America have an operative model of the universe. It may be a cosmic vault upheld by a tree on whose out-reaching branches gods and spirits dwell . . . or a hierarchy of supernatural entities each of whom exerts a particular influence on the world.

Similarly, the Qabalistic Tree of Life and the symbolism of the Major Tarot Trumps constitute the operative universe of the Western magician. This framework delineates the symbolic layering of energies within the magical unconscious. The framework asserts: the gods of mythology are inside the mind . . . they are themselves a programme. To re-enact the programme is to encounter the gods of the Western tradition, in a certain sequence which is indicative of their sacred power.

If we look at the twenty-two cards of the Major Arcana from *The World* through to *The Fool* in this way we can detect a process of transformation occurring in the impact of the symbols themselves. The *World* and *Judgement*, for example, are clearly cards of entry. The Persephone symbolism of *The World*, the dancing maiden within the wheat wreath — the polarity of life and death as possibilities, the Eleusian promise of spiritual rebirth and awakening — all of these are indicative of greater things to come. Persephone herself was snatched down through the earth into the underworld . . . in modern terms a transition from the real to the unconstricted dimension of dreams.

The 'higher cards' of the Major Arcana, like *The Emperor* and *The Charioteer*, *The Hermit* and *The Hierophant*, are all faces or facets of the great male archetype, just as the *High Priestess* and *The Empress* are embodiments of the great White Goddess before and after procreation.

The Western magician believes that by visualizing the cards inwardly so that they in fact become alive — an inner living process — he is activating archetypal energies. The magician is also introducing a crucial component of the shamanistic act, the concept of *altering consciousness under will*.[1] The magical act is not arbitrary — it is made in the spirit of command. The Western magician knows the scope of his hierarchy of gods and goddesses, his spirit allies and archangels, and when he invokes them he does so within a symbolic confine which defines the space of their activity. He may seek their uplifting energy by invoking them into his own body, but he is very conscious of what he is doing, and imposes the symbolic 'limits' of the effects he is unleashing. The path inward is carefully constructed. Randomness is indicative of a lack of resolve and, in the medieval sense, an invitation to possession — not in terms of an attack by wilful spirits or the devil, so much as dominance by powerful images which impress the explorer by their 'reality'. The magician treads warily through his inner heavens and hells. His weapons are sacred mantras or god-names which within his own 'programme' are of profound significance. The name of a god is superior to that of an elemental by virtue of their very positions in the magical hierarchy. The magician's weapons also include the skilful use of the imagination. Shamans in the West have long known that the imagination is itself a form of direction — it can lead one into wonderful and awesome spaces that are both illuminating and terrifying.

Once again, the shaman in the West employs imagination subject to will. He imposes upon the vast range of visual and auditory possibilities that occur in the hallucinatory world of the lower unconscious, a particular set of images. He follows the set of Tarot symbols not because of their literal value, but because they are internally consistent. They are a visually expressed programme for expanding consciousness through archetypal levels. This provides the magician's sense of certainty. He knows the milestones of his inner territory. It follows that we should not become too entwined in debates concerning the relative validity of Gautama Buddha's eight-fold path compared with the ten Qabalistic sephiroth, or argue about the colours ascribed to the chakras in yoga and in Western magic. There is no escaping the fact that there are minor differences. What is more pertinent is that once we opt, for reasons of temperament or cultural preference, for one particular system, we should abide by the language of its symbolism. In mystical systems we are dealing with elaborate metaphysical metaphors which have implied but not literal validity. Each person has the right to follow his own programme.

There has been much romantic speculation concerning the origin of the Tarot cards. Most commonly the cards have been linked with the gypsies of Central Europe, although the *tarocchi* cards are known to have been present in Italy a hundred years before the incursion of the gypsies around AD 1400. Paul Christian exemplifies a commonly held occult belief that the Tarot cards of the Major Arcana formed a symbolic rendition of an ancient Egyptian initiation rite supposedly held in vaults below the Great Pyramid, and the French theologian Court de Gebelin argued similarly that the word 'Tarot' itself derived from an Egyptian phrase meaning 'royal road of life'.[2]

While it is quite apparent that Tarot symbolism is very much a product of the medieval world-view, with its armoured warriors, castles and ornate costumes, it is also true that whereas the Tarot has no apparent historical links with the earlier cultures of the ancient Near East, and classical Greece and Rome, it does nevertheless embody a similar attempt to explain metaphorically the essential mystery of man's being.

We have stressed that as a system of entry into the psyche the Tarot takes a major place because, as will be shown, the symbols of the twenty-two cards represent a process of transformation. The shaman opening the doors to these energy levels finds himself unable to resist transforming also, as he comes to embody the spiritual energies inherent in each level.

There were, however, *three* programmes of entry to out-of-the-body consciousness in the Golden Dawn, and as a prelude to describing the Tarot symbolism it is appropriate that we should also consider the other related systems, namely those of the so-called Tattvas and Enochian symbols.

The Tattvas

These are the Hindu symbols of the elements, and represent one of the few Eastern sources of Western magical technique. They are named as follows:

Tejas, a red equilateral triangle	Fire
Apas, a silver crescent	Water
Vayu, a blue circle	Air
Prithivi, a yellow square	Earth
Akasa, a black or indigo egg	Spirit (the Void of Space)

43

The magicians of the Golden Dawn used these symbols for focusing on the mythological spaces defined by the elements, both as individual symbols and in combination. The motifs were mounted on white cards and the magician stared concentratedly at the symbol before averting his gaze to produce an after-image. This was then used as a meditative centering through which to enter the astral planes.

Several visionary accounts of this form of trance entry survive in what have been called the Flying Rolls, documented by Francis King.[3] They usually take the form of encounters with angelic or elemental beings, each said to belong to a specific 'realm' and resemble those described in the earlier section which dealt with the cosmology of Franz Bardon. The visions are frequently of earth spirits, sylphs of the air, undines, fire-beings or a combination of these.

The Enochian Squares
While the Tattvas provided an alternative means to the Tarot for entering 'inner space', they were individual paths of entry, rather than *a series of symbolic states which would lead to the transformation of the magician himself.*

The visions of the so-called Enochian system of magic also allow similar scope, but again the magician ventures inward through an isolated elemental doorway, rather than embarking on a shamanistic journey through a series of archetypes.

Historically the system derives from a series of communications in the trance state involving one Edward Kelley, and Queen Elizabeth I's astrologer, Dr John Dee. Kelley and Dee employed a number of ritual devices in order to contact certain angelic beings in the 'spirit vision'. The angels appeared in a crystal or 'shewstone' and appeared to point with a wand to certain letters which equated in turn with a set of large squares filled with figures of the alphabet that Dee and Kelley had themselves drawn up. The angels dictated certain powerful 'calls' or conjurations, and these, together with four of the major squares, were used by the magicians of the Golden Dawn as aids for venturing on to the astral planes.

The four major tablets of letters were ascribed to each of the four elements. There was also a smaller fifth tablet containing rows of letters which were interpreted to be the god-names of the elements, for example:

EXARP-Air; HCOMA-Water; NANTA-Earth; BITOM-Fire

A special method of pronunciation was also employed.

The magical method of 'projection' was to select a specific square within the much larger tablet and visualize it three-dimensionally so that it became a truncated pyramid. Each square would have different combinations of elemental and zodiacal influences bearing on it, and the visions produced in the out-of-the-body state were accordingly a complex mix of symbolism. They were made more elaborate again by the Golden Dawn practice of visualizing Egyptian gods surmounting the pyramids. Isis was said to be predominantly a water goddess, Horus, one of fire and Osiris of spirit. Anubis, on the other hand, the well-known guardian of the dead, was a combination of air and earth. Other deities were ascribed up to three elemental 'components'.

One such was Ahephi, one of the children of Horus, and said to embody fire, water and earth. The following record of a Golden Dawn astral encounter demonstrates the principle that the vision is a symbolic resultant of the elements of entry:[4]

> Formed pyramid over me. Went through it . . . and saw Ahephi in the centre of the brilliance, and himself light and white . . . I said I wanted to interview the Sphinx of the pyramid . . . I saw him easily and at once but his colours were not brilliant. I asked him to explain to me the forces to which he corresponded, beginning with the universal force he represented.

> *Answer:* I represent active forces acting between the waters above and the waters below the firmament dividing the waters and energized by Fire . . . you may see it in Nature in the weather, where the Fire and Air keep the upper and nether waters apart. It represents a cloudy atmosphere with a sea below, but the air between is dry and in active motion; there is no chance of rain, nor is there much evaporation from the surface . . .

This is not a record of the complete vision, for the magician concerned later had an encounter with a symbolically attired angelic being and surveyed the surroundings from the top of the pyramid. My point in quoting it, however, is that the contents of the vision square closely with the elements ascribed to the doorway of entry.

The occult secrets gained from the supernatural entities, the god, the sphinx and the angel, are hardly profound, and are in a sense quite predictable.

We can regard the Tattvas and the Enochian squares as useful symbols on which to focus the imagination. The symbols come to life in the visionary state as the magician enters the astral plane of the creative psyche. But the point I would like to make here is this: it is not so important that the visions represent embodiments of various elements — what is far more crucial is what I would like to call 'the span of consciousness' allowed by each symbolic encounter.

A magician concentrating on a symbol of fire meditatively, will produce visionary results of fire, and with earth, results of earth and so on. But such a symbol constitutes a limitation, a confinement of the senses. He is bound by his symbol of entry, for this symbol determines the 'span of consciousness' possible in the circumstances.

The Tattvas and the Enochian squares are thus restricted because in each instance they are individual and unconnected paths of entry into the symbolic realms of the psyche. They do not allow the magician to expand, as it were, once he is in the trance state.

The system of the Major Tarot Arcana is, however, more far-reaching. Here we have a series of pictorial images, which allows the shaman to journey from one inner landscape to another. He grows through the succession of visual encounters and enlarges his domain by virtue of his meeting with the deities of the Tarot pantheon. His span of consciousness is unlimited because the Tree of Life framework is itself open-ended.

Richard Cavendish has written:[5]

> The Golden Dawn's method of meditation on Tarot cards was well calculated to produce the intended effects. The meditator had an idea of the significance of each trump and its path on the Tree to begin with, and he knew the 'correspondences' — the gods, animals, plants, colours and the rest — which expressed its nature. . .

Cavendish implies in this remark that the Golden Dawn approach was somehow invalid — it pre-empted itsown results. It seems to me that we need to consider the Tarot from another angle, however. The more familiar the magician is with the Tarot symbolism, the more real it can become imaginatively on the astral plane of the creative imagination. If it then triggers archetypal experiences because of the validity of the symbolism as a sequence of magical images, then the method has proved successful. Clearly the magicians of the Golden Dawn were not finding absolutes inside their heads — they were following, or even imposing, a system of magical images as a particular programme to be followed. What is far more important is the span of consciousness allowed within the programme. There are twenty-two cards of this mythological domain of the Tarot and I will discuss each one in turn, my emphasis being on the Tarot as a growth series rather than isolated symbolic representations.

The shaman who uses the Tarot cards as his doors of entry to the unconscious mind, enters with the card of *The World.* This card, while ostensibly feminine — a dancing maiden within a wreath of corn — is actually latently hermaphroditic, for the figure contains both sexualities.

The shaman traditionally enters through a doorway, a subterranean tunnel, or through a gap in a rock-face, and comes upon the sacred territory which medieval lyricists called faerie-land and which other cultures have called 'the vault of the heavens' or depicted as a journey upon the sacred tree. The Tarot card of *The World* leads out of Malkuth on a direct vertical ascent, and in this sense the magician who takes this path is, in a very real sense, beginning to climb the Qabalistic Tree of Life.

There are two other paths of entry: *Judgment,* which leads to the left hand side of the Tree and the sephirah Hod; and *The Moon* which leads to Netzach. These paths symbolize different aspects of the human temperament. Hod is more the rational, intellectual sphere which mirrors in a lesser form the constructive, uplifting and maintaining role of Thoth/Zeus/Jupiter — the overseer of the heavens. The Hod-Mercury link pertains to the messengers of the gods — an early card in ascending through the pantheon of archetypal energies.

Judgment shows figures holding their arms aloft in tribulation at the call of Gabriel's trumpet. They are reborn, re-awakened to the inner psyche. But the key here is the vibratory mantra, the very essence of being in magical philosophy which actually causes regeneration. We re-awaken according to our capacity to receive.

The Moon like a number of cards, presents a 'triangular' aspect to the sephirah Yesod which it mirrors, that is to say it appears directly opposite Hod as a path. It is a feminine, lunar card, ruled by the Moon which watches carefully over the evolutionary aspects presented to view. We see an emerging crustacean, the evolution of the wild wolf into the domestic dog, man's symbols of dominance — the castle and parapets — in the distance. Once again we glimpse the structure of the natural order but the clear direction is towards the sky, the vault of the cosmic order beyond man as he is in the unregenerated state.

Yesod links with the genital regions of microcosmic man and typically indicates the animal, sexual instincts: the region of the inner man called *Nephesch* by the traditional Qabalists.

Two cards lead out of this sphere to each side of the Tree, once again in a 'balancing' divergence — one to Hod and the other to Netzach. One is solar, the other lunar — *The Sun* and *The Star* respectively.

Again the cards relate to energy sources in the vicinity: *The Sun* to the solar archetype of Tiphareth — again the triangular relationship — and *The Star* to the lunar archetype of Yesod.

Yesod is one of the domains of the White Goddess. We will meet her again in her two roles, the aloof virginal goddess, and the proud and fulfilled Mother of Creation. Diana and Hecate are also aspects of this energy source and *The Star* depicts a beautiful naked maiden kneeling in the waters of spirit, and pouring their life-providing energies onto the earth below. This card mirrors *The Magus* — the virginal magician at the top of the Tree who transmits in like fashion the power of Kether down its entirety. The seven minor stars in the sky seem to focus on the central power source (Kether/the Trinity) and to surround it in the same way that the seven lower spheres on the Tree represent the seven 'days' of Creation.

These cards, then, are representative of growth, awakening and emergence. In *The World* and *Judgment* we are reaching into the psyche. *The Star* shows that fruitful intuitive energies flow from an inner, sacred source at a quite early stage of the shaman's journey.

The Sun is similarly transitional. The Sun, resplendent in its golden intensity dominates the top part of the card, but the young children who play in its radiance are not yet fully grown. Shamanistically they are young upon the journey, and we will find them depicted again later in *The Lovers,* where they have matured, and in *The Fool,* where they have fused hermaphroditically beyond sexual division.

We have now completed an early cycle of growth through the Tarot symbols which requires consolidation through the first of the 'horizontal' cards upon the Tree, *The Tower.* We are immediately aware of the relation of this card to the *Nephesch* for it is especially phallic. But there is a profound lesson incorporated in the card, which is that *The Tower* also symbolizes the human framework. The body of inner man has to be internally balanced and well-structured if it is to withstand the lightning flash from Kether which will strike its turrets destructively unless the shaman is able to transform it. There are hints too of the vanity underlying the Tower of Babel. The shaman must tread warily. His personality will undergo transformation as he journeys higher. But the first lesson is that his pride and his ego must be left behind.

The card which takes the shaman beyond this domain is a card of balance and evolution once again — *Temperance*. On Aleister Crowley's rendition of the card we are shown an angel stirring a cauldron — a universal shamanistic symbol — and fusing therein all the elements of which man is mythologically composed. On Paul Foster Case's version of the same card we see a sun rising between two mountains in the background beyond the archangel of fire — a hint that the god-energy, the Kundalini, is rising in the shaman himself if he can attain it.

Raphael is almost like a guardian; he is awesome and impressive with his vessels of fire. But he protects the worthy and symbolizes strength and inner preserve.

Temperance leads to Tiphareth, which is a vital part of the Tree. We have here the hub of the inner mandata, the centre which mythologically is described as the sun around which the planets of the zodiac rotate — a prime symbol of balance and harmony. It is the first major initiation for the shaman. He emerges from the cauldron of forthcoming as a warrior regenerated by the spirit. He is fortified against the demonic imagery of his lower unconscious and he will be able to proceed now on two quite harrowing paths, *Justice* and *The Hermit*.

It is important to note that Tiphareth is a card of transition rather than an end in itself. Osiris and Christ were both solar gods of transition, bridging a gap between man and the very source of creation. The mystic seeks to enter that undifferentiated source of being which has been variously described as *satori*, *nirvana* and *cosmic consciousness*, a domain in which the individual and the universal have become One, and Tiphareth points the way to this exalted state.

Two dramatic cards adjoining Tiphareth show that one of the great shamanistic myths unfolded at this stage is the death/renewal process. We find here *Death* (Netzach-Tiphareth) and *The Devil* (Hod-Tiphareth), both of which show in different ways man coming to grips with his 'lower' nature. On *Death* an angry skeletal figure wields a scythe above a crop of human heads and broken bodies. But we notice that beyond the field of carnage a river flows into the sun, and it is clear that Death removes the limiting and unwanted aspects of the human personality — pride and arrogance and so on — and like *Temperance* exerts a restructuring effect. *The Devil* is the last attempt of the psyche to exert a sense of ego in the animal domain. The Devil sits triumphant over a man and woman whose bestial aspects are crudely shown by horns, tails and cloven hoofs. They stand shackled to his throne . . . a reminder that they are trapped by their desires and immediate passions.

The Devil is however a blind; he is the negative face of Tiphareth which can trap the shaman not prepared to journey further. In the sense that Lucifer-Satan was a fallen god he is also a transitional figure, and his kingdom serves as an outer court to the domain of the inner sun.

Justice and *The Hermit* further fortify the shaman on his journey. *Justice* demands brutal self-assessment. We find the polar opposite — the loving and enticing Venus here — for now she holds a threatening sword ready at any moment to cut away self-deception, arrogance and falsehood. The lunar cusp on the sword indicates that she is the White Goddess in yet another guise, and she too represents transition; beyond her domain and shielded by a veil, is the land of the great gods of the higher regions on the Tree.

The Hermit depicts what various mystical traditions have called the Dark Night of the Soul. The Hermit trusts to his inner voice for guidance but he travels alone upon the dark, icy slopes of the cosmic mountain. His ego is diminished now; he wears the robes of anonymity and is beginning to awaken to the wisdom of The Ancient of Days (Chesed) in whose direction he climbs.

If *The Hermit* and *Justice* are both powerful cards of rigorous self evaluation, *The Wheel of Fortune* and *The Hanged Man* are cards of encouragement. *The Wheel,* which again mirrors the mandala-like effect that Tiphareth exerts in the centre of the Tree, depicts a universal vortex of life energies. On the other side of the Tree, meanwhile, we find *The Hanged Man,* who in a very appropriate way, is more clearly thought of, not as a murdered villain, but as a reflection of a higher principle. Much has been made of the symbolism of what purports to be a crude sacrifice on a wooden edifice. *The Hanged Man,* like *The Wheel of Fortune* does of course mirror the death-renewal or resurrection-rebirth concepts which are integral parts of the Tiphareth energy vortex and crucial to all solar myths including those of Apollo, Dionysus, Osiris and Christ.

The Hanged Man, who is best depicted mythologically in the Thoth pack of Aleister Crowley, reflects the watery domains of the great Ocean of Spirit (Maris — the virgin sea, the great Mother of Form) and as such is a beacon to the world below — a very appropriate mythological function which the historical Christ performed in the world during his incarnation.

We come to the second horizontal card upon the Tree at this stage: *Strength*. It is interesting that, whereas the traditional Qabalah is very much dominated by the different faces of the great male archetype, the Tarot card which unites Geburah (Strength) and Chesed (Mercy) is one depicting the Great Mother. Feminine intuition and grace dominate an angry lion, symbolic of the final victory of higher thought over the animal instincts inherent in lower man.

It is at this stage that we have really begun to pass beyond the animal kingdom — man's traditional domain — altogether. The final cards are renditions of very powerful inner spaces, awesome energies which owe far more to the basic spirit of the cosmos than to man's individual perceptions.

In a shamanistic sense, the remaining Tarot cards really attempt to depict a transcendental process almost beyond imagery. However, the magical shaman requires milestones on the sacred inner territory and these cards are, in this capacity, an inner structuring of his journey, which takes him through the vault of the heavens and wards off the Qlippothic elements of chaos which are present at all stages on the Tree of Life.[6]

As mentioned earlier, *The Lovers* depicts a more evolved form of the energy level represented by *The Sun*. On *The Lovers* we see the young maiden and her youthful escort moving towards a state of inner union. Love produces a state of balance and, more importantly, *totality*; the sense of transcendental completeness which is of course appropriate to Kether — the sourcepoint of all creation. Love in itself is very much an attribute of the Great Mother (Binah — *The Empress)* who gave birth to them, and the card is a journeying home towards the Source.

The love of the divine son and the divine maiden (Tiphareth and Malkuth) is mirrored on yet a more exalted level by the polar contrasts of *The Empress* and *The Emperor*. These are the great archetypes overviewing creation and take the function in the universe called the Demiurge, the maintainer and overseer of what has in itself emanated from a more subtle, unformulated level.

If we regard the living universe as a source of energy forms, some of which are manifest in growing organisms and others resident in forms which have outlived their usefulness, it is clear that any mythological set must depict the polarity of growth and destruction. We find the merciful, maintaining role in the card of *The Emperor* especially. He is Zeus and Jupiter, the great father archetype who watches benignly over his domain and subjects below. But his other face is destructive and in the Tarot it is represented by *The Charioteer* who unlike the stable, stationary Emperor seated on his stone throne, moves actively and vengefully through the universe of form. He is the warrior (Geburah -Mars) whose purpose it is to destroy and eliminate growth forms which are themselves impeding the evolutionary process.

The Charioteer mirrors the energy of the Great Mother/Ocean of Being in the sense that he is a warrior of water (he bears a crab as an emblem on his helmet) and also holds as his weapon not a sword, but a mirror — for he is the all-seeing eye. Once again, the Crowley Thoth cards depict this process most accurately. The more familiar Waite — Case packs by contrast lack the vital sense of motion and activity which distinguishes this card from the more passive symbolism of *The Emperor*.

The Hierophant, which like *The Emperor* is aligned to Chokmah, is similarly a face of The Ancient of Days, the arbiter of spiritual wisdom in the universe. But he also represents a principle that Church institutions in the present day occasionally forget, namely that spiritual authority derives from inner experience. In this sense a priest or Church father should hold his post because of his ability to transmit inner knowledge to his congregation.

The occult revival and the diminishing of Christian influence in particular is no doubt related to a human craving for archetypal recognition — we all need the mystical experiences of inner reality. The contemporary prevalence of gurus indicates a widespread need for people to follow those who claim to embody in different ways the inner light. *The Hierophant* incorporates in its design the somewhat heretical suggestion that the Pope should also be a mystic — a prospect that historical Christianity has not condoned.

The three remaining cards of the Tarot-shaman's pantheon of images are *The High Priestess, The Magus* and *The Fool.* If we bear in mind that one mythological means of representing a pure state of being is by depicting the archetype as virginal (totally beyond blemish, a symbol of transcendence) then *The High Priestess* and *The Magus* are the virginal equivalent forms of *The Empress* and *The Emperor* who 'know' each other by virtue of their bringing forth the offspring of Creation.

The High Priestess sits beyond a veil of mist, an ethereal distant rendition of the White Goddess who, in a lower form, was more active in the world of images. But *The High Priestess* is totally withdrawn — her domain extends vertically on the upper half of the Tree of Life, beyond the Abyss which cleaves the Tree into essence and form. In the symbol of *The High Priestess* we have a transcendental and almost unknowable form of the White Goddess.

Similarly in *The Magus,* we find a male archetype who is already subject to the androgynous aspects inherent in Kether. He is not masculine in the sense that *The Charioteer* or *The Emperor* are. His face is soft and feminine, and although his act of transmitting magical inspiration down the causeways of the Tree is an act of power, his authority is inherent rather than felt. His symbols are clear — he manipulates the wand and sword of masculinity, and the cup and pentacle of femininity, which will later become forceful motifs in the creative imagination. But he is hardly a figure in the world of actuality; he too is transcendent.

Finally, *The Fool* depicts a most precarious state of being. *The Fool* is a young virginal person whose sexuality is deliberately unclear, and who hovers between the manifest universe and the Void beyond Form. The shaman at this stage undertakes the final journey. The card invites him to pass beyond form into the undifferentiated state of universal bliss, the infinite and ineffable state of unity and mystery described by the traditional Qabalists as *Ain Soph Aur,* the limitless light.

It is evident that the Major Arcana of the Tarot hardly belong with the other fifty-six minor cards at all. Mythologically they represent a growth process thematically absent from the 'lower' cards, which depict the elemental division into fire, earth, water and air and all its permutations.

While traditional scholarship has rejected the recent suggestion that the Qabalah and Tarot are mutually reinforcing, there is no doubt that quite aside from historical considerations of origin, the two systems together form a very effective shamanistic programme. We discover in the cards, as we enter at the level of earth consciousness, that the shamanistic flight of ecstasy potentially traverses the entire inner universe of the creative imagination.

The Tarot cards are used specifically as a basis of visualization, and the required method is to become sufficiently acquainted with the symbolism of each card so that it can be imagined in full detail at the dictate of the will. The magician thus conjures it into appearance as part of a sequence of symbolic locations which define his venture into inner space. The venture may be undertaken meditatively but it is far more 'real' when combined with the out-of-the-body experience.

Three Tarot packs are commonly available which owe their formulation to the Golden Dawn and allied systems of magic and we have referred to them already. These are the Rider pack designed by A. E. Waite and Pamela Coleman Smith; the BOTA pack of Paul Foster Case and Jessie Burns Parke and the Thoth pack of Aleister Crowley, illustrated by Lady Frieda Harris.

The first two of these are relatively traditional and portray the symbols of each card in a decorative rather than an experiential way. The Thoth pack, however, is designed very much to portray the actual magical reality and symbolic domain of each card, and as a set they are much more a part of the tradition of visionary art than any other existing pack. We need to remember, however, that they are also tinged by Crowley's personal magical world-view, and certain aberrations are present in their format. After his sojourn in Egypt, Crowley actively switched his allegiance from ceremonial to sexual magic and from this time onwards defined his shamanistic identity in terms of the Egyptian pantheon of gods and a somewhat garbled rendition of the anti-Christ account found in *The Book of Revelation*. For example we find *Strength*, which normally depicts a maiden overcoming the brute strength of a lion, replaced instead by *Lust*, and showing a rather indulgent scarlet lady, the Whore of Babalon, revelling on the back of a multi-headed, atavistic chimera.

Nevertheless, in a visual sense Crowley's pack is our basic point of commencement for the shamanistic tradition in the West. The following meditative descriptions are built on the basic symbolic content of each card and offer a visual summary of each doorway. Accompanying each description is what I have called a 'technique of passage' — a means of confronting the mythological imagery and responding to it.

The World

A naked maiden dances joyfully in a wreath of wheat. She also hold two wands, one in each hand, and the Hebrew letter Tau, meaning salvation, swirls around her body like a mantle. At the four corners of this symbolic entry through the earth are the four apocalyptic creatures *of The Book of Revelations:* man, bull, lion and eagle.

Technique of passage: The wreath of wheat defines the outer limits of a tunnel or vortex through which the shaman will enter. Regard the dance of the maiden as symbolic of the interplay of creative energies in all creation.

Judgment

The angel Gabriel, with golden hair and a dazzling blue robe holds forth a long stemmed trumpet, and its resonant, melodious sound causes seemingly dead figures to arise from graves with their hands uplifted. The coffins surprisingly float on water and this sea is really the ocean of spirit of the Great Mother. A banner depicting a red cross on a white field, symbolic of rebirth, is attached to the neck of the trumpet.

Technique of passage: Rise up on the waves of sound, identifying with the vigour of rebirth which the trumpet proclaims.

The Sun

Two young and innocent children dance at the foot of a grassy hill. A brick wall separates the children from its peak while a radiant, golden sun fills the sky with its brilliance. Sunflowers growing on the wall entice the children to grow toward the light.

Technique of passage: Enjoy the recovered sense of innocence with your young partner of the opposite sex. Feel the waves of sunlight reaching down, playing on the skin, yet drawing you into the energy vortex which is the Sun itself. Respect the sanctity of the domain beyond the wall for it is a sacred place.

The Moon

The lunar crescent dominates the sky and sends down showers of silvery light particles upon the kingdom below. Two dogs, one wild and the other tame howl at the sky; a lobster struggles out of the water onto the bank, battling against the limitations of its form. Man's castle turrets, grey and built of heavy stone, reach up to the sky as a symbol of his dominance of nature.

Technique of passage: Reflect on the evolutionary processes that you see before you — the struggle of the lobster to evolve into a land-form shape, the metamorphosis of the wild, brutish dog into a more refined domestic creature, the place of man in the natural domain. Regard the silvery moon-pellets as a dew, a subtle life essence which fertilizes and makes more complete the dominating energy of the sun.

The Star

A beautiful naked maiden reaches up to the sky with a silver goblet and captures the fructifying essences of a night-star. These flow through her as if she were a translucent, glass vessel and well up into a cup she holds in her other hand. She empties the life-giving fluids onto barren earth. The landscape is resplendent in a pearly grey and mauve half-light. When the maiden moves, the atmosphere seems to shimmer like liquid silver.

Technique of passage: Enjoy the sensation of entering into the process of the transmission of spirit and life-force from one vessel to the other. Re-live the process of subtle essence manifesting in an earthen context.

The Tower

A fierce bolt of lightning strikes and crumbles the stone battlements of a lofty tower. Chunks of masonry, a golden crown which surmounted the tower, and two unfortunate human beings, hurtle earthwards. The sky is ablaze with violent, all-subsuming red and orange flame and a vengeful eye can be seen in the centre of the angry heavens, surveying the vanity of man in trying to build a tower to reach skywards.

Technique of passage: Feel the electric discharge in the air and endeavour to identify with the ruined tower while imagining that at the same time it enlarges itself into a more strongly fortified dwelling, capable of withstanding the wrath of the lightning bolt. Regard your body as a tower which has to be built on sound foundations with no inner conflicts of intent. The tower itself is now raised anew with humility and respect for the energy sources which sustain the universe.

The Devil

Two degraded human beings with horns and tails stand chained to a stone pedestal on which perches the grotesque form of the horned Devil. He has eagle's claws and bat's wings, and a goat's head surmounted by an inverted white pentagram. His body is fleshy and coloured earthen brown and the presence of a breast suggests that he is in some degree hermaphroditic. He holds a torch downwards in his left hand and his right is held open as if in mock salute.

Technique of passage: Encounter the Devil but reflect on his incongruous nature; he is an absurd idol of worship which makes all the more tragic the plight of other human beings chained to his command. Dwell on the imagery of the Devil's face and, realizing that it is a mask which conceals a greater inner reality beyond its outward pretences, feel yourself passing through the hollow cavities of the eyes.

Death

A frenzied skeleton wielding a scythe dances insanely through a field of human heads. Scattered carnage litters the ground but the spirits of the dead merge and flow into a river which wends its way through a valley into the land of the inner sun. The skeleton is an ashen grey colour, the sky is flaccid like a heavy, pervasive liquid suggestive of astral forms.

Technique of passage: Allow your body to be hewn to pieces, identifying at the same time with the greater, spiritual personality which is released from bondage, and which will now flow with the tides of the spirit. Regard 'death', at this stage, as a process of refinement.

Temperance

A golden headed angelic being with enormous outstretched, shimmering wings stands in the stream of Life with one foot on the ground, and one in water. His gown is pure white and a radiant golden disk shines from his forehead. Above him a beautiful rainbow spans the sky.

In his right hand he holds a flask, and he pours water from it onto the head of a scowling dusky lion who lies subdued near his right foot. In his other hand he holds a blazing torch, whose flames shower onto the head of a silver eagle.

Beyond the angel a sun can be seen rising between two mountain peaks and the stream is seen to flow down from this more elevated source.

Technique of passage: Regard the angel as a spiritual being who provides a profound sense of inner balance. He represents the fusion of the elements into a state of harmony and the stability he offers is a requirement of entry into Tiphareth, the sphere of the Sun which lies just beyond the mountain peaks.

The Hanged Man

A young man wearing red tights and a blue jacket whose pockets bear emblems of the moon, hangs upside down from a wooden gallows. The gallows are in the form of the Hebrew letter Tau and he is attached by his right leg, with a rope, to the cross-beam above. His hands are clasped behind his back out of vision but make a triangular shape with his body. His left leg meanwhile is bent, forming a cross with his suspended right leg. The focal point of attention, however, is the man's head which shines like a beacon, emitting an illuminating radiance. The atmosphere is watery as if, in one sense, the hanged man is a reflection in a rippling pool rather than inverted in his own right.

Technique of passage: Imagine yourself drawing near to the beacon which is the hanged man's head, and then merge with it so that you begin to reflect the light which he is transmitting from above. Reflect on the sacrifice which the subtle inner light has to make in penetrating denser matter and inwardly thank the figure of the hanged man for acting as an intermediary between matter and spirit.

The Wheel of Fortune

The giant cosmic wheel, the pivot of the manifested universe, turns on its axis amid tides of energy which disperse to all corners of the universe. The ten-spoked wheel is golden in colour and is surmounted by a vigilant sphinx bearing a sword who remains stationary at the crest of the wheel as it turns purposefully beneath him. A yellow serpent coils itself around the left hand side of the wheel and the Egyptian jackal-headed god resides on the right hand. Once again the four creatures of *Revelations* — man, eagle, bull and lion — are present in the four quarters: all golden in colour against a blue sky.

Technique of passage: The Wheel of Fortune is itself a mandala, a symbol of infinity. Concentrate on the centre-point, the focus of the eternal process of unfoldenment: and pass through it regarding it once again as a symbol of transformation.

The Hermit

A bearded sage stands holding a lantern in which shines a six-pointed golden star. He carries a staff in his other hand and wears a full-length cloak of dark grey. Gradually he traverses the rocky, icy path on the side of the mystical mountain of created being. He is a lone traveller, very much guided by the illumination of his lantern.

Technique of passage: This card teaches us to trust the guiding inspiration of the inner self, the Holy Guardian Angel. Reflect on the anonymous quality of the sage's appearance, the absence of outwardly expressed individuality. Identify the lantern as an image of the self and become more firmly resolute in the upward climb to the peak of creation, where individuality will become increasingly less important.

Justice

The White Goddess of Justice sits enthroned in a temple radiant with silver and blue light. In her left hand she holds the scales in which she will weigh the spiritual qualities of all who come before her. Her two-edged sword, with a hilt consisting of lunar crescents, is a symbol of impeccable authority. Her hair is golden, her robe red and her cape green. She is the warlike aspect of Venus, and guardian of the sacred territory of golden light which lies beyond the confines of her temple.

Technique of passage: Following the process of refinement and self-transformation that we found in *Death*, allow yourself to be judged impartially by *Justice* and submit to her trials. Realize that it is in fact the loving side of the higher self that sits in judgment and that only illusions and inconsistencies will be ruthlessly disbanded.

Strength

A woman with a wreath of coloured flowers in her hair stands silhouetted against a yellow sky, restraining the anger of a red lion. Her cloak is pure white and she wears red roses around her waist. The lion is clearly subservient to her for she places roses around its neck too.

Technique of passage: Identify with the forces of intuition and patience inherent in controlling the animal instincts which are at the core of all human activity. Become the woman of the flowers and take her place, holding in check the primal energies of the lower self.

The Charioteer

A warrior with golden armour, his helmet bearing the insignia of the crab and his elbows adorned with lunar crescents, rides in a chariot drawn by two sphinxes, one black and the other white. The roof of his chariot is vivid blue flecked with stars and the wheels and body of his carriage a warlike red. He holds in his hands a mirror in which he sees, in the manner of an all-perceiving eye, the unwanted aspects of Creation which are ripe for destruction.

Technique of passage: Assume the role of the warrior and imagine the mirror reflecting inwardly on yourself, in an act of rigid self-scrutiny. Enter into the sense of flux which is the process of life and death itself, and regard the warrior not so much as a wanton destroyer but as a scourge of unconstructive and conflicting elements which stand in the way of inner unity.

The Lovers

An angel wearing a violet robe and with arms outstretched sanctifies the two lovers, who stand naked in a state of innocence regained. Behind Eve is the Tree of the Knowledge of Good and Evil bearing five fruits; a serpent coils around its trunk. Behind Adam resides another tree whose fruits are twelve flames — each with three tongues representative of the signs of the Zodiac. A golden sun illuminates the sky above the angel and in the distance of the far horizon we see the mystical mountain showing its peak.

Technique of passage: This card represents the fusion of sexual polarities in the self, a further transformation towards union beyond duality. Consequently the basic impact of this symbolism is recognizing and fusing lovingly with the complementary sexual polarity, embracing the other aspect of one's masculine or feminine nature.

The Hierophant

The High Priest sits on a grey throne fashioned from stone. His robe is red, edged in green, his blue undergarment visible as he raises his hands. He wears a triple-layered golden crown and holds in his left hand a golden staff with three cross-bars near the top. His right hand is uplifted, bestowing blessings. His shoes are white and are inscribed with crosses, and near by, lying crossed on a red carpet, are two keys: one silver (lunar) and the other golden (solar).

Technique of passage: The Hierophant embodies spiritual authority but simultaneously bestows grace on those who have ears to hear. Again he represents the gradual fusion of solar and lunar principles.

The Emperor

The Emperor sits on his throne carved from a cubic stone, surveying the kingdom of manifest creation. He holds in his right hand a wand surmounted by the head of Aries the ram, and the same motif appears on his armour. In his left hand he holds a globe surmounted by a cross, and he is seated with his left leg crossed over his right, the cross in both instances symbolizing the figure four (Chesed: Mercy — the fourth sephirah). Except for his white beard, the vision of the Emperor is dominated by the colour red, the colour of Mars, which rules Aries. The Emperor is facing towards the left and we see only his profile: he is a form of the Ancient of Days.

Technique of passage: The Emperor, although a merciful aspect of the Great Father archetype, is approached with respect. He should nevertheless be regarded as in some ways unfulfilled — his kingdom is barren without *The Empress,* and he owes as much to her as *The Hanged Man,* who similarly had his legs crossed in the sign of four, and also reflected the Great Ocean. The shaman passes from the rocky, mountainous kingdom of the Emperor to the more welcome and abundant pastures of the Empress.

The Empress

The Empress is the Great Mother of Creation. She sits on a throne in a field of wheat, a row of cypresses in the background. Her robe and dress are russet and green — colours of the earth — and her hair flows down her shoulders in long golden swirls. In her right hand she bears a heart-shaped shield inscribed with a dove, and in her left, a sceptre bearing a globe surmounted by a cross. A silver crescent is visible beneath her foot and twelve silver stars shine around her forehead. Near by, the River of Life pours down upon the crops providing irrigation for a fruitful harvest.

Technique of Passage: The Empress is the supreme representation of Mother Nature, the great womb of all manifested forms, and to encounter her is to return to the very source of created being. It is a reaffirmation of the process of life and fulfilment itself, the home of the River of Life. The shaman surrenders himself to the source of his form.

The High Priestess

The High Priestess sits on a stone throne beyond a sheen of silver mist. She wears a lunar crown and a shimmering blue cloak which falls, in folds suggestive of water, to the temple floor. In her hand she holds the scroll of memory, and on her breast she wears an equal-armed cross. Her manner is cold and aloof; she is the supreme virgin goddess. On her right side stands a black column and on her left a white one, Between these is a veil which renders invisible the sacred territory beyond Ccreation.

Technique of passage: The shaman here enters sublime, virginal ground: the very essence of the Universe before its fall into form. This region is the first symbolic domain which will take him undifferentiated into the Void of Space.

The Magus

The Magician holds his wand aloft, receiving the energy of the prime creative impulse, and with his left handpoints downwards towards the direction of the manifest universe. He is the supreme transmitter of energy but resides, himself, above basic forms. His cloak is red, his bodice pure white. Around his waist is a coiled snake swallowing its tail. The Magus has before him the four symbols which are the language of creation: the cup, the pentacle, the sword and the wand. His domain is filled with golden-white brilliance.

Technique of passage: The magus is the male virgin who has not had contact with the female polarity in order to reproduce and bring about form. He is pure energy and like the High Priestess remains transcendental and essentially unknowable.

The Fool

The Fool represents the Supreme Mystery. He is depicted as a youth, perhaps male, perhaps female, about to step over a cliff into the Vvoid. The Fool's outer garment is floral and multi-coloured, incorporating numerous solar mandala motifs and a single silver star. The inner garment is a pure dazzling white.

The expression on the face of the Heavenly Androgyne is one of high indifference — the balance between force and form, between male and female, being fine and precarious.

Technique of passage: Within the shaman's journey, this is the supreme path, in which the magician dissolves his very being in the void of the final mystery.

We have considered at length the shamanistic implications of the Tarot as a series of inner visions. The god-energies which they lead to in the psyche are vortexes of considerable authority and creative impact. They are such that they transform the shaman on his journey.

However we should consider not only the 'span of consciousness' opened by the Tarot but also the reasons for its internal balance, the harmony resident in its very structure when superimposed on the Tree of Life.

The God Levels

We have described the gods as symbolic representations of energy states. They depict the forceful interaction of the intellect, intuition and emotions, and they characterize our instincts and passions.

David Miller in his *The New Polytheism* writes:

> We are the playground of a veritable theatre full of Gods and Goddesses. What do the Gods and Goddesses want with us? Our task is to incarnate them, become aware of their presence, acknowledge and celebrate their forms so that we may better be able to account for our polytheism.[7]

The Qabalistic levels are tenfold and reflect the traditional Judaic patriarchal consciousness although the addition of Tarot symbolism in the modern context has, significantly, restored the balance of polarities.

The Ten Sephiroth are:

Kether
Chokmah
Binah

Chesed
Geburah
Tiphareth
Netzach
Hod
Yesod
Malkuth

In the traditional mythological sense these levels on the Tree are:

Neutral
Male
Female
Male
Male
Male/Neutral
Female
Male
Female
Female/Neutral

There are several methods for testing the internal balance of the Tree of Life and the Major Tarot Arcana. From the mythological viewpoint the Tree appears as in Figure 2.

Method 1: Polarities at levels
Binah and Chokmah are polarities of feminine and masculine, but both emanate from the Void of Space, *Ain Soph Aur*, which resides above duality. The alchemists depicted this state by means of a symbol of a king and queen joined together.

Binah and Chokmah represent the first division into form and force; the second division into a major polarity occurs at the next level between Geburah and Chesed where masculine aspects represent, once again, force and form.

At the next stage of descent Tiphareth is the masculine product of the union of the Great Father and the Great (virginal) Mother of Heaven. Tiphareth is in the centre of the Tree like the focus of a wheel, the centre of a mandala, and is appropriately represented by the Sun. The Sun gives life and accordingly is masculine (force aspect) but its position is on the 'middle pillar' which provides a tendency towards neutrality. It is interesting that most depictions of the mythological Christ — as one example of the divine son — show a very

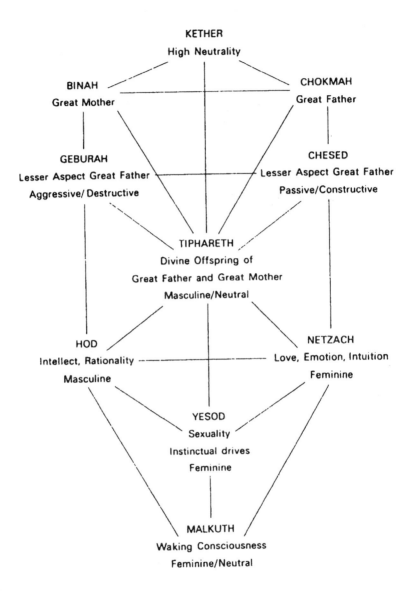

Figure 2

feminine and not all aggressive form of masculinity in which internal polarities are resolved.

At the next level Hod and Netzach balance as polarities of attitude, one an attitude towards the objective, the definite and the measurable, the other a tendency towards the subjective, the intangible and the emotive.

Yesod as shown by its position on the Tree, resides over the genital region. It is the sphere of all the sexual drives of man.

There is a growth sequence in these levels from animal-man through to God-man and thence to the states of infinite consciousness beyond form itself. Any avatar incorporates the midway state of cosmic consciousness in the human body. ('No man cometh unto the Father' is thus a correct statement in the mythological sense.)

Malkuth is the offspring of the divine parents with a feminine aspect, but she too has tendencies towards androgyny. The first and last cards of our sequence both have hermaphroditic qualities, following the occult axiom: 'As above, so below.'

Method 2: Colour polarities
The Tree of Life consists of ten levels of consciousness. These, however, can be divided mythologically into the white light of the 'Trinity' — the three supernals at the top of the Tree — combined with the seven colours of the rainbow.

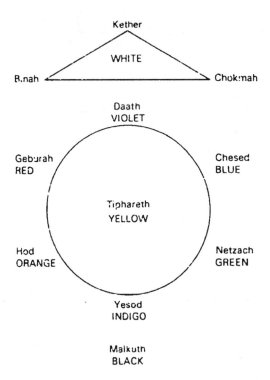

Figure 3

In so doing we separate Malkuth, the state of earth-consciousness from the Tree (which, in the system of chakras, is black in contrast with the white light from the top of the Tree) and we introduce the so-called 'eleventh sephirah', Daath. 'Daath' means knowledge and is ascribed to the Tree midway between Kether and Tiphareth. The Tree of inner man now appears as in Figure 3.

Viewed in this way, the Tree of Life which usually looks especially linear, acquires the property of a mandala containing all the qualities of the rainbow. The shaman who integrates its qualities within his being will indeed have acquired all the attributes of white light. The wheel of inner colours, meanwhile, is exquisitely poised between light and dark and the growth of consciousness is reminiscent of the ancient Gnostic concept of escaping from darkness to light.

The magicians of the Golden Dawn, as with exponents of yoga, ascribe the energy levels of the Tree to what in the East are called the 'chakras' of inner man.[8]

The chakra-equivalents in magic follow the pattern of the diagram, so that the colours visualized by the magician who is endeavouring to 'bring down the light' of *Ain Soph Aur* into his own being follow the pattern from Kether down to Malkuth:

White — Violet — Yellow — Indigo — Black.

Meanwhile from the viewpoint, yet again, of internal balance, the remaining colours form two sets of complementaries in a cross upon the Tree:

Red — Green
Orange — Blue

Method 3: The 'dominant' Major Arcana on the Tree of Life
We observe an interesting effect in terms of polarity when we analyse the Tarot ascriptions upon the Tree in terms of what I would like to call 'dominant' cards.

It is clear that several of the Major Tarot Trumps reflect quite directly the symbolism of the sephirah which lies opposite on the Tree in a 'triangular' relationship. For example, both *The Hanged Man*, who is 'crucified' and also shines as a beacon to the world, and also *The Wheel of Fortune*, each show different aspects of Tiphareth. On the one hand *The Hanged Man* is an archetypal variant on the sacrificial saviour, the reborn solar gods like Osiris and Christ, while *The Wheel of Fortune is* a mandala which reflects Tiphareth's position in the centre of the Zodiacal Tree. Other examples of this 'triangular' situation, in which the card reflects the meaning of the sephirah, are *The Sun, The Moon, The Lovers, Justice* and *The Tower*. Several other cards, notably *The World, The Star, The Hermit, The Charioteer, The Hierophant* and *The Fool* very strongly reflect the sephirah they are *linked to.*

Quite apart from this consideration, however, it is possible to take each of the ten sephiroth, and to isolate 'triads' of Tarot cards which lead out from each of those sephiroth in an evolutionary direction. It is necessary to stress that we are considering the symbolism only of those cards which represent *growth upwards,* for this reflects the true shamanistic purpose. (Several sephiroth on the Tree, of course, have triads which reach downwards.)

The pattern of triads which emerges can be shown as follows:

MALKUTH   World — Star — Moon (Right-hand side)
                       Judgment — Sun — World (Left-hand side)

YESOD   Temperance — Death — Star (Right)
                       Sun — Devil — Temperance (Left)

HOD   Devil — Death — Tower (Right)
                       Hanged Man — Justice — Devil (Left)

NETZACH   Tower — Devil — Death (Right)
                       Death — Hermit — Wheel (Left)

TIPHARETH   High Priestess — Fool — Emperor (High right)
                       Emperor — Hierophant — Hermit (Lower right)
                       Lovers — Magus — High Priestess (High left)
                       Justice — Chariot — Lovers (Lower left)
                       Lovers — Empress — Emperor (High centre)
                       Justice — Strength — Hermit (Lower centre)

GEBURAH

CHESED   No evolutionary triads

BINAH

CHOKMAH   Identical triad:
                       Magus — Fool — Empress/Empress — Magus — Fool

KETHER   Upwards beyond the Tree, a triangle whose invisible sides are infinite!

What I will call the 'dominant' Major Tarot cards in this arrangement are those Arcana which occur in both couplets (in the case of Tiphareth due to its position on the Tree we have three pairs of couplets).

The dominants which now emerge are: World — Temperance -

Devil — Death — Lovers — High Priestess — Emperor — Empress — Magus — Fool, that is a total of ten, the number of sephiroth upon the Tree. But more significantly, when evaluating the Tarot as a programme for inner space, the 'dominant' cards are perfectly balanced in terms of structural polarity.

On the Tree the 'dominants' align as follows:

	Fool
Higher Tree	Magus
	Empress
	Emperor
Middle Tree	High Priestess
	Lovers
	Death
Lower Tree	Devil
	Temperance
	World

The polarities of these dominant Tarot cards can in some instances be identified as masculine or feminine quite easily. Several of the cards, however, exhibit a fusion of the sexes — *The Fool, The Devil* and *The World* all depict androgynous creatures, and *The Lovers* shows the gradual fusion of sexual opposites. Other cards depict a different sort of neutrality: *Temperance* combines all the elements in a balanced totality and *Death*, which depicts a skeleton, is necessarily sexless!

We are now in a position to assign a polarity:

	Fool	Neutral
Higher Tree	Magus	Masculine
	Empress	Feminine
	Emperor	Masculine
Middle Tree	High Priestess	Feminine
	Lovers	Neutral
	Death	Neutral
Lower Tree	Devil	Neutral
	Temperance	Neutral
	World	Neutral

This procedure of identifying the dominant cards demonstrates a vital point in assessing the Tarot as a shamanistic method, namely that its structure is internally consistent. We find that the Tarot ascriptions have in a sense re-balanced the heavy patriarchal tendency which was to be found in the traditional Qabalah. Even these cards which exhibit a definite mythological polarity balance beautifully: we have the virginal male and virginal female *(The Magus* and *The High Priestess)* counterposed by the Great Father and the Great Mother, whose union produces the universe *(The Emperor* and *The Empress)*. From the shamanistic viewpoint the pantheon of supernatural beings reflects an ordered universe. The programme, in John Lilly's sense, is a balanced one.

From the equally important viewpoint of colour, the shaman, as with the Jivaro Indian who journeys to the gods in the land of coloured mists, here literally finds himself confronted with a rainbow circle whose totality is white light. His journey takes him through all the colours of the cosmic mandala.

4
Surrealism and the Qabalah

Mythology has often interwoven itself with art but never with such variety as in the art of the surrealists. Surrealism and Dadaism constituted an early attempt by a notable group of visionaries to extend reality beyond its confines. André Breton sought in automatic writing and spontaneous art a means of overcoming the meddling interference of the intellect, a direct route into the creative unconscious — a fusion of dream and reality.

It is not surprising that many of the surrealists, notably Dali, Delvaux, Ernst, Lam, Tanguy and Magritte exhibit mythological incursions in their work. Surrealism sought to uncover new vistas of the imagination and it is reasonable to expect that if the Tree of Life framework with its mythological images were to have any claim whatever to representing a matrix of symbols of the Western psyche, these archetypes would manifest strongly in surrealist painting. The actual surrealist methods also bear strong comparison with those of Western magic.

Anna Balakian notes that in following the theories of Freud the surrealists found in automatic writing a form of 'self-administered psychoanalysis; placing themselves in a state of stupefying attentiveness, they tried to shut out all outside disturbances and to give free play to the inner powers of association of words and the images which these suggested . . . '[1]

As we have already seen, the contemporary magician similarly withdraws his attention from the external world to a meditative dimension where his language is one of ritual names of power and specific symbols, like Tarot arcana and Tattvas, for focusing the attention. The source-work 777 represents a body of associated mythological images arrived at by much the same process as that found in surrealism. One important difference, however, remains the concept of will.

Automatic techniques require a total openness in the practitioner. The magicians of the Golden Dawn were given to structuring their inner journeys and employing protective techniques comparable to those found in yoga. The surrealists, and their latter-day disciples, the supernatural realists, nevertheless share an aspiration which is also a hallmark of the current consciousness movement — a broadening of vision, an inquiry into the sources of inspiration and man's neglected powers of creativity, and a refusal to abide by the consensus logic of the day. The early Dadaists and Surrealists were revolutionaries in the true sense. Dadaist exhibitions were on occasion closed by police on the grounds that these new manifestations had nothing whatever to do with art.[2] Indeed, this period was host to a new vision which proposed to destroy the *status quo* by shattering it out of its complacency. The method of the new movement was undoubtedly anarchistic, but it was one of good-humoured insights — a challenge to the senses.

J. H. Matthews in his *Introduction to Surrealism* notes that 'the surrealist sees humour as the conjunction of the real and the fantastic; not only helping man resist the claims of the reality to which the world has accustomed him, but also placing within his reach the means to shake off habitual thought, thus permitting him to aspire to another form of reality, which answers another logic'.[3]

If the surrealists themselves found amusement in the way in which they demolished all faith in representational reality, the reaction of their audience was sometimes one of not taking the new art form too seriously. Hugh Philip, in a 1944 edition of *Angry Penguins*, wrote: 'Surrealism is just a trick; quite a clever trick at times, but nonetheless a trick, which in this day of uncritical admiration, almost worship of the new, the original, the bizarre, has "caught on" . . .'[4]

From our current standpoint it is now apparent that the surrealist mode which was, as Julien Levy put it, *a point of view*, has not been eclipsed by later fashions but has remained as one of the dominant styles in modern art. The graphic collages of Wilfried Satty and the supernatural realism of Viennese artists like Ernst Fuchs owe much to Max Ernst. Magritte's tamperings with physical perspective have found their way into numerous counter-culture graphics, among them the cover illustration for Carlos Castaneda's second volume *A Separate Reality*, and the works of Gervasio Gallardo, a contemporary fantasy illustrator. Modern advertising art shows that the visual effects evoked by the surrealists continue to prove effective as a means of arresting attention. Surrealism in fact achieves its result by appearing to represent an unfamiliar reality. Like contemporary forms of magic, surrealism takes us into locales where a new logic applies, where a new combination of images and symbols is presented in its own right. Matthews notes:

> The objects and creatures surrealism creates must impose themselves upon the imagination with all the conviction of truth — Ernst's hundred-headed woman, Breton's soluble fish and white-haired revolver or those strange encounters recorded so faithfully in the canvases of Delvaux, Magritte, Dali or Dorothea Tanning. The Surrealist invites his public to look before he asks them to understand. And he takes care to compel them to look, as dreams do, even when they have no expectation of understanding what they see. Thus the Surrealist — whether painter or poet — becomes in Eluard's phrase 'a slave to the faculty of seeing'.[5]

The way of the modern shaman is to journey through the landscape of images knowing that they are as real as he wants them to be. He may become ensnared in hells expanded by his own fears and paranoia, or he may be entranced by heavenly visionary states of great beauty and splendour. The shaman can journey through symbolic locales which lead to his own transformation. The surrealist achievement was to indicate — for the first time with force since Bosch and Cranach — that reality extends to these domains, that the imagination encompasses all possibilities.

Several surrealists exhibit identifiable mythological content deriving from various archetypal energy sources, and accordingly express the surrealist world-view through different motifs and effects. It becomes possible to propose a three-fold division of the mythological images relating to the basic cosmology of earth, moon and sun.

For Magritte, the magic vision lies in rearranging an otherwise familiar reality so that flowers or pieces of fruit occupy a whole room or heavy objects float serenely in space, defying gravity. His orientation is Qabalistically associated with the physical world of Malkuth, and his technique hinges, like that of de Chirico, on perspective, shape and visual contrast.

Delvaux, Tanguy and Dali meanwhile emerge as predominantly lunar painters in the Qabalistic sense. Delvaux is the most obvious of these. Naked maidens walk through his pictures in trance-like reverie beneath the moon; his pictorial themes invariably revolve around the image of the White Goddess. Delvaux's nudes are milky-skinned, aloof, unblemished and often accompany death in the form of a skeleton.

Sexual, serpentine trains pass near by but are never linked in any way to the frigid, silent women.

Tanguy meanwhile has made the symbol of the ocean one of personal significance. The moon is linked Qabalistically to the element water. Tanguy grew up in a mystical domain himself — the village of Locronan near the legendary Ys, which was said to have been engulfed in the fifth century when the daughter of King Gradlon formed an illicit love pact with the devil and opened the flood gates protecting the city from the sea. As a youth, Tanguy used to dive in the sea in search of bones and pebbles washed by the waves and there is a strong sense in his paintings of an ocean of hidden inner imagery. Tanguy's surreal landscapes are often lunar grey and filled with an apparently reflected light such as that which has filtered through to the bottom of the ocean. His more elastic shapes have a suggestion of mutability to them, and in like fashion the lunar region of the unconscious, the Yesod of the Qabalists, suggests an ocean of forms and images constantly, like the tides, in a state of flux and transformation.

On the basis of the microcosm and macrocosm, the Tree of Life is also the Tree of Man (Adam Kadmon) and Yesod is superimposed upon the region of the genitals indicating that it also refers to the sexual impulses and fertility (another aspect of lunar worship, in witchcraft, for example).

While much of Salvador Dali's work is dream-like and elastic in quality (incorporating dripping clocks and pliable bodies), it is also extremely sexual. His *Young Virgin Auto-Sodomized By Her Own Chastity*, for example, involves a double play of images so that the young woman's limbs become aggressive penises. Marcel Jean has said of Dali's paintings that several are appropriate as 'illustrations of a kind for a still unwritten manual of psychoanalysis: even the titles sometimes provide a commentary with Freudian undertones. A predilection for suggestive or even remarkably unsymbolized sexual themes is noticeable in his work.'[6] Freud himself regarded Dali as the most significant of the surrealists, and their world-view hinges around the same primal sources in the unconscious.

While it is true that these surrealists — Tanguy, Delvaux, Magritte and Dali — to a large extent remained true to a dominant mythological energy source, the work of Max Ernst appears to embody marked transitions. His early work, such as that characterized by *The Elephant of the Celebes* (1921) is noticeably mechanistic, mirroring the Dadaist revolt against technology and its effects. Later paintings depict the savage forces inherent in Nature and his work comes to represent a powerful, atavistic vision of man embroiled in Nature's grasp. The last twenty years of Ernst's life, however, see a refinement of the harshness in his earlier work, and suggest a new-found calm. The mandala, a symbol of individuation or wholeness, features predominantly in his work, and suggests a centering absent for much of his artistic career. In Ernst's paintings, as with the medieval alchemists, we find a merging of opposites, of animal and human, of male and female. Even his mandala representations have two polarities; Paul Waldo-Schwartz in *Art and the Occult* makes the interesting observation that 'Ernst's suns are never wholly suns at all but equally lunar disks. They reflect rather than radiate, and end up as sigils of the great Zero wherein the solar-lunar, male-female union is mysteriously combined.'[7]

In the Tarot sequence we recall that the consciousness domain linking Yesod and Tiphareth, the lunar and solar centres, is represented by *Temperance*. This Tarot arcana represents a fusion of the elements, a gathering of resources and a harmonizing of influences, very much characteristic of Ernst's later work.

Malkuth is the Qabalistic entry into the unconscious mind and there is no doubt that of the transformers of physical reality towards a magical end, René Magritte is the supreme exponent. Magritte himself believed that painting was a magical act, and that the painter was endowed with superior powers. It has been said of him that 'Magritte behaves like God. He makes fire burn without consuming, puts boulders in the sky, pins clouds to the ground, turns men into stone, makes stone birds fly, forbids us to look upon his face . . . '[8]

The motifs and representations in Magritte's paintings are familiar but his use of them is not. In *The Tomb of the Wrestlers* an evocative pink rose fills a room, and in *Personal Values* a huge comb and shaving brush rest on a miniature bed and wardrobe while leaning against the bedroom wall which is the sky. Magritte is able to shock us out of our everyday awareness by counterposing images: the face of a bowler-hatted man is obscured by an apple, while other such men are shown fashioned from clay and living in a world which is totally earthen. Elsewhere toes grow out of boots and breasts are superimposed upon a dress. Magritte is similarly a magician of context. In *The Childhood of Icarus* a jockey rides his horse through a large room in which there are framed pictures of the sky and the external face of a building. And true to defying gravity, Magritte depicts a huge boulder supporting a fortress floating carefree in the sky while waves below lap upon a beach *(The Castle of the Pyrenees)*.

Magritte has said that magic is explicable only when it is utterly inexplicable, and his paintings bear this out. In *Ariadne's Thread*, Magritte stressed that he also viewed his approach as akin to poetry:[9]

> . . . assuming as real the poetic fact, if we try to discover its meaning we find a new orientation which immediately removes us from that barren region that the mind has ceased to fecundate. The object of poetry would become a knowledge of the secrets of the universe which would allow us to act on the elements. Magical transactions would become possible.

Among Magritte's magical images are a mermaid consisting of a women's legs and the head and torso of a fish, a bird filled with sky, and a man seated at a table — his head ablaze with white light.

The latter picture, *The Pleasure Principle,* recalls the magical technique described in Carlos Castaneda's *Teachings of Don Juan,* of transferring consciousness under willed imagination, to the head.[10] Like Carlos Castaneda, Magritte was a city shaman. George Melly of the BBC described him in 1965 as a secret agent, bent on bringing to disrepute the whole apparatus of bourgeois reality. 'Like all saboteurs,' said Melly, 'he avoids detection by dressing and behaving like everybody else.'[11]

While Magritte offers a magical interpretation of our familiar physical world, and in this sense is very much a painter operating within Malkuth consciousness, certain pictures embody a notion of implied transcendence. *The Glass Key* is very much an earthen landscape depicting an isolated boulder positioned on the top of a heavy mountain ridge. The picture is enthralling because it suggests that the boulder is breaking with its origins — transcending its own state of density and pointing aspiringly to the heavens.

Also, it should be noted that while Magritte deals in the language of physical images, he does occasionally betray his mythological interests. *The Musings of a Solitary Walker* shows a man strolling beside a river, but in the foreground we are shown a figure deep in a somnambulistic trance, strongly reminiscent of beliefs concerning the human double. David Sylvester has referred to the intrusion of Egyptian influences on *L'Homme du Large* which depicts dream images like hieroglyphic inscriptions on a tomb, and in a fauvist painting, *The Image of the Hermaphrodite* — itself a mystical symbol of union — we are shown the bearded ocean god with a penis in the form of a woman.

In the work of Delvaux, Tanguy and Dali we find evidence of a preoccupation with different aspects of the lunar consciousness of Yesod, whether represented by astral, dream-like imagery, portrayals of the White Goddess of lunar worship or strongly sexual allusions. Delvaux's women are usually entranced, as if sleep-walking. They are often naked, in procession, and convey a sense of magical ceremony. They walk beneath the moon, linked, it has been suggested, only by silence. For Marcel Jean, 'these women in lace gowns moving towards a triumphal vista of ancient buildings are all the same woman, duplicated, multiplied by invisible mirrors.'[12] We are never quite sure where we stand in Delvaux's pictures; his women especially seem aloof and withdrawn. We are not invited to participate in their ritual.

Delvaux insists on bringing his mythological women, however reminiscent of ancient Greece and Rome, into the twentieth century. *The Acropolis* and *The Cortege* both show processions of semi-clad maidens bearing lamps. Temples are visible, but other buildings are shown illuminated by gas lamp lighting. In *The End of the World* a group of young women stand on a pier overlooking a moonlit lake. Nearby we notice a solitary railway carriage, suggesting that the mythological journey has come to an end.

Other works also show a fusion of traditional and contemporary world-views as if Delvaux is actively seeking to bring a magical awareness into the technological era. In *The Trolley, Red Door, Ephesus,* a tram courses its way along a street flanked by ancient temples, and whilst the trees which flourish in Delvaux's dream-time are in a natural setting, in *Christmas Night* trees grow near a railway yard in rows of pots. The woman perusing this scene is clothed, and in the context of Delvaux's other work, seems to be caught between the world of technological normality and a desire to act mythologically by shedding her clothing and regaining the status of a lunar wanderer.

In several of Delvaux's paintings Death takes a hand in the form of a skeleton. The latter is a bizarre metaphorical image of the 'inner man'. In Delvaux's view normal human beings are death-stricken, while skeletons are expressive with their gestures. Persephone-Hecate and the Roman Diana are also associated with death, and Yesod is the first station in the underworld of the unconscious mind. It is not surprising that we find the death skeleton accompanying Delvaux's lunar worshippers in works like the famous *Sleeping Venus.* Delvaux deals in the polarities of life and death, classical and contemporaneous, sacred and profane, dream-like and physical. He invites us to expand our sense of causality by allowing both dimensions to occupy common ground, and proposes that the classical mythological sensibility be born again in each of us.

The paintings of Yves Tanguy, by contrast, are not overtly mythological — they invariably depict smooth stylized objects and beings which have presence rather than personality — but they represent other facets of the lunar consciousness. Tanguy's symbols and motifs seem very much to suggest transition — objects becoming more real and requiring the creative mould of the ocean of formation upon them. His landscapes, in the lunar sense, are subject to the tides, and owe their very essence to the ocean, which as we have seen, is a basic cosmological image of spirit, space and causality. And while his early paintings like *The Mood of Now* and *With My Shadow* (both completed in 1928) have a definite organic feel to them and include limp fibrous growths and stem-like motifs, Tanguy's more mature works are markedly more abstract. James Thrall Soby has described his paintings in terms of the 'melting of land into the sky'[13] — Tanguy's flaccid forms seem to arise in an aspic dimension and often float in space, like newly conceived ideas.

Yesod is the energy source upon the Tree which pertains to this aspect of the creative process. Through it forms and images are channelled into the psyche en route to their final manifestation in Malkuth. The Tarot card *The Star*, which depicts the White Goddess with two flasks, transmitting the essence of a star into the waters of life upon the earth, is similarly suggestive of the current and flow of creative ideas. In Tanguy's *A Large Picture which is a Landscape* (1917) we already have a clear preference for lunar greys, and the light in the picture is diffuse. In *The Lovers* his figures are rather like plasticine ghosts, with little shape or distinctiveness, and in the centre of the composition ambiguous shapes hover, free-form and unattached. The astral imagery of Tanguy's inner domain is characteristically shown in *The Rapidity of Sleep* where the planar objects join together almost like a sequence of memories from waking consciousness and taper off into a void of forgetfulness in the distance.

On the Tree of Life, the sephirah which flows into lunar Yesod is Hod, an energy vortex which supports the concepts of structure and form, and in particular stimulates rational design and mathematical formulation. Tanguy, while invariably elastic in his textures, nevertheless brings considerable structure into his later works, and in this sense appears to be interpreting the forces of Hod in a lunar context. *Indefinite Invisibility* (1942) sees a newly found mechanistic quality, reminiscent of science fiction machines which exhibit a positive structure but an elusive function, and the dolmen-like objects of *The Closing Days* are metallic in their sheen, rather like statues guarding the kingdom of an unknown intelligence. Tanguy elaborated his sense of intricate structures in works like *Rose of the Four Winds, The Transparent Ones* and *The Hunted Sky,* where his motifs are suggestive of hieroglyphics that etch themselves onto his object-shapes like a mysterious growth. *Multiplication of Arcs* was Tanguy's crowning work, and one which is unmistakably lunar. The landscape is populated by crowded rock formations, suggestive both of natural forms, and also a pervasive intelligence.

Tanguy, true to the lunar sense of transformation, never allows himself to be pinned down to a specific expression, with only one level of meaning. In his work we find a language of symbols which raises the paradox of their origin, and leaves us pondering the void from which they appear to precipitate. His later paintings, in quite a different way from that of Delvaux, nevertheless share that artist's sense of profound silence. Tanguy's horizon images gesture upwards into grey mysterious skies which taper off into another dimension and invariably his paintings seem lit with reflected light, enhancing fissures, textures and shadows. His is not the humanized expression of mythological archetypes but suggests instead their abstract qualities. Tanguy's later works are unquestionably 'hopeful'. His textured sentinels seem to await the dawning of a greater reality, and it is appropriate that his final painting, *Multiplication of Arcs,* saw the most complete expression of his mysterious images made manifest.

Dali meanwhile, drawing on the traditions of Flemish art and psychoanalysis simultaneously, rendered his images with more distinctiveness than Tanguy, and arguably with less mystery. Despite his dream images, Dali always had one foot in reality. He once proposed an experiment in which a colossal loaf of bread, fifteen yards long, would be baked and left early one morning in a public square in order to stimulate widespread incredulity. His so-called 'paranoia critical method' is based on visual puns, with the physical environment finding itself subject to hallucinatory interpretation. Like Magritte, Dali was a master of surprise, and had similarly taken it upon himself to fracture all sense of a bourgeois consensus reality. In a letter to Gala Eluard, later to be his wife, he wrote: 'I believe the moment is at hand when by a paranoiac and active advance of the mind, it will be possible (simultaneously with automation and other passive states) to systematize confusion and thus to help to discredit completely the world of reality.'[14]

Dali read Freud's *Interpretation of Dreams* and this revealed to him the whole dimension of repressed obsessions, neuroses and complexes which impinge on everyday behaviour. Dali was impressed by Freud's method of dream analysis as a means of expanding one's understanding of hidden aspects of the personality, and he became increasingly interested in insanity as an alternative world-view, much in the same fashion as R. D. Laing and Wilson Van Dusen.[15] In his painting The *Invisible Man* Dali built his dream images meticulously, and they in turn formed a suggested, or hidden image of the man himself, thereby 'giving pictorial expression to the way the insane impose double meanings on reality'.[16]

Like Magritte, Dali's shock effects invoke imagery from the physical world — the Qabalistic Malkuth — but his dream images are both elastic and hypersexual, characteristic of lunar Yesod. The sense of a fluid, astral dimension is very much apparent in works like *Hercules lifting the skin of the sea asks Venus for one moment longer before she awakens love* (1963). Hercules lifts the surface of the sea like a film and all the figures seem to be set, as if in a dream-like jelly. Dali's own *Soft Self Portrait* is a plasticine mask, propped up on crutches, and *The Great Masturbator* exhibits not only elasticity, but marked eroticism. A woman's head and a man's genitals emerge from an amorphous plastic/organic sculpture; it is very much a case of the dream made tangible. In so many of Dali's works one can feel the texture, catch hold of the culprit image which is the key to parallel dimensions.

Paintings like *The Temptation of Saint Anthony,* with its bizarre insect-elephant processions, and *One second before awakening from a dream caused by the flight of a bee around a pomegranate,* characterize Dali's living nightmare. Yesod is the astral realm of dreams and memories which pertain to the individual ego. We have only begun to impinge on a more universal archetypal consciousness in these pictures. On Dali's own admission, his work relates primarily to the subconscious of the individual and, true to Freud's direction, dwells more with individual repressions and neuroses rather than any transcendental Jungian notion of a Collective Unconscious.

Dali's religious phase produced his most shamanistic painting. In *Santiago El Grande* the Christian hero mounted on the cosmic horse rises towards the vaults of the crystal heavens. Christ appears transfixed in space and radiating light, some distance above him. This particular excursion into supernatural realism very much epitomizes the new direction which has since emerged in the mid-1970s — the search for a powerful spiritual mythology and its artistic depiction in realistic and non-abstract images.

There have always been magical elements in surrealism as a result of the visionary journey into the unconscious, and the artist's meandering in the forest of symbols. We think of Victor Brauner's paintings teeming with occult familiars, Felix Labisse's animal/human transformations and Wolfgang Paalen's totemic landscapes. Wifredo Lam, in particular, has embodied in his work the concept of the unconscious as an infinite source of awe and wonderment which can inspire the artist to great heights. He had seen the fantastic images of Bosch and Bruegel in the Prado after leaving his native Cuba for the first time in 1923. In 1940 he joined the Surrealist Movement, and after its dispersion (Dali, Tanguy and Ernst to the United States, Paalen to Mexico) Lam returned to Cuba. He visited Haiti four years later and was initiated into the voodoo ecstasy cult of Vevers. The voodoo practitioner seeks to elevate his spirit to the level of the *loa* divinities, to embody their uplifting energies through the act of physical possession. Lam demonstrates in his work the common ground occupied by visionary art and magic. He has been a wanderer among the spirit beings who dwell deep in the jungle of the human unconscious, a shaman worshipper among both devils and divinities, gods themselves half human, half vegetable, and very much images of transformation. Lam has said of the forest that it represents 'that world without limits with the mystery of its space indefinitely prolonged beyond the veil of its tree-trunks and leaves'.[17]

Lam's personal cultural heritage was enormously multi-faceted. His mother was a mix of African, Indian and European, his father Cantonese. From his contact with surrealists onwards he came to stress the nature of his art as an expression of the inner journey, and allied his pictorial techniques with that of automatism — direct and unimpeded contact with the unconscious. 'In my canvases', he once said, 'I transmit all that is essential in the interior of my being.'[18]

This being so, we discover a vast range of images and forces lurking in the psyche of the Cuban surrealist. Horned, bird-head humans with fierce teeth, claws and daggers, warrior steeds, creatures with ritual gestures who blend back into the forest having appeared for an instant, totemic insignia — all of these throng his paintings, and have made works like *The Jungle* and *The Eternal Present* justly famous. Lam's paintings have extraordinary force, and his graphic interest in ritual sigils, especially those found in Voodoo ceremonial, flow into his compositions so that they become an invocation in their own right. Lam's painting of the Voodoo god of thunder, Oggum Ferraille (or Ogoun Feraille), draws on personal visions derived from Voodoo techniques of ecstasy. His conviction that at 'a level of the mind deeper than the reasoning faculty desire awakens'[19] is reminiscent of the surreal English trance artist Austin Spare, one-time disciple of the occultist Aleister Crowley. Spare, like the Voodoo practitioners, entered trance states in which he would deliberately seek union with the hidden atavistic images of his mind — in his case images he believed to be animal memories of a previous incarnation.[20] Lam, like Spare, constantly portrays the human transforming into the animalian, or fusing with the branches and foliage of the jungle. His art is alive with totemic images illuminated, like Tanguy's paintings, by a diffuse ethereal light.

Like Lam, Max Ernst — among the most cosmic of the surrealists — had recourse to the symbol of the forest. However, while much of Lam's preoccupation was with visually invoking the spirit forces which lurk therein, a recurrent theme in Ernst's work has been transcendence. His sympathy was with the bird, another highly personal symbol, who rises above the melange of Nature spirits and demons and takes refuge in the sun.[21]

Ernst, like Tanguy and Lam, grew up in a magical, evocative environment. He was intrigued by the vastness of the Black Forest, which seemed to him to represent an infinite dimension and a great source of hidden mystery. The noted medieval occultist Cornelius Agrippa wrote his famous treatises in Cologne, only six miles from Ernst's birthplace, Bruhl, and when he was nearly fifteen an event occurred which for Ernst was truly magical. His pet pink cockatoo died suddenly, and almost immediately a sister was born into his family. As a result of this synchronistic occurrence, Ernst became deeply interested in occult matters; it seemed to him that he had witnessed a type of transformation.

Ernst's early compositions are highly mechanistic. *Winter Landscape: The Asphyxiation* (1921) shows pipes and furnaces beneath the level of the ground throwing pollution into the air and causing the branches of a tree to wither. His famous *Elephant of the Celebes* is a mockery of ugliness — his monster being a grotesque, furnace-like creature devoid of any aesthetic function. Its neck lunges forward like a dangling pipe, its tusks are misplaced and its legs resemble truncated stumps. The creature responds to a gesture from a headless human being.

Ernst soon heeded the call of the forest and its bird life as basic visual images of his response to the environment. True to his Dadaist reaction against technology, his *Little tear gland that says tic tac* does include a representation of the forest but his sun is a tooth-edged metallic gear wheel. As a reminder that many of the forces of Ernst's psyche were still trapped from full expression, his *Dove* (1928) is depicted behind the bars of a cage.

Max Ernst soon embarked on a number of pictures which showed both the dynamism and destructiveness inherent in Nature. In *The Joy of Living* we are shown luxuriant vegetation, but on closer examination discover anthropomorphic creatures lurking there, one with pointed human fingers and sharp needle teeth. Several works show a solar or lunar disc transcendent over a putrefied earth, *Grey Forest*, and a number of paintings entitled *The Entire City* in particular. A gradual direction emerges in his artistic career towards identification with the disc or mandala itself, a symbol of the reconciliation of opposing forces both within the mind and the external environment.

Ernst had a visionary approach to creativity from an early time in his life. He notes in *Beyond Painting* that since the age of five he had been able to exercise a remarkable capacity for seeing more than would normally be apparent to the casual observer. A wooden panel painted with black strokes on a ruddy field to imitate mahogany provoked what Ernst has called 'associations of organic forms (a threatening eye, long nose, huge bird's head with thick black hair)'.[22] In August 1925, while resting in an inn at Pornic near the sea coast, Ernst gazed down at the accentuated grain of the wooden floor boards and excitedly began to take tracings of the grain with a soft pencil. 'I was surprised,' he writes, 'at the sudden intensification of my visionary faculties and at the hallucinatory succession of contradictory images being superimposed on each other with the persistence and rapidity of amorous memories.' Later he explored other materials and textures — leaves, cloth, thread — 'my eyes perceived human heads, various animals, a battle ending in a kiss *(Bride of the Wind)*, rocks *(The Sea and the Rain, Earthquake, The Sphinx in her Stable)*.'[23]

The textural surfaces on which Ernst fixed his gaze became for him a leaping-off point, a catalyst to his imaginative endeavours. In this sense they resembled the sigils upon which Austin Spare meditated while entering a state of trance, for they too were catalysts to an amazing outpouring of energy from the unconscious.[24]

Ernst named his process frottage, and he found that gradually the specific textures became subordinate to the images which manifested through the process. He had discovered a way of rendering invisible potencies tangible in the light of day. Like Spare, Ernst referred to forces operating through him — 'the method excludes conscious mental guidance . . . reducing to a minimum the active part of what has hitherto been called the "author" of the work.'[25]

For Ernst, the artist was not an originator so much as one who is present at the birth of his work. And like the magician, with profound respect for the forces and images inherent in the vast archives oil the mind, Ernst saw his role as requiring direct entry into the symbolic inner domains which would inspire him:[26]

> . . . every normal person (and not only the 'artist') carries in his subconscious an inexhaustive supply of buried pictures and it is a matter of courage or of liberating methods (such as automatic writing) to bring to light from expeditions into the unconscious unforged (uncoloured by control) objects (pictures) . . .

Ernst's philosophy quite clearly embraces the shaman's world-view. The surrealist journey is into inner spaces and dimensions which will yield powerful and expressive images of a greater reality. Like the shaman's direct sojourn with the gods of his culture in a quest for meaning, Emst was similarly engaged in finding 'the myth of his time'.[27]

The Robing of the Bride (1939) remains one of his most impressively occult paintings and depicts semi-human creatures who seem intent on a macabre esoteric ceremony. The central figure — the bride herself — wears an owl's mask, suggestive of transformation into animal forms, and her richly textured robe is highly ritualistic. A bird-headed man nearby holds a menacing sword and a curious four-breasted amphibious creature (the anticipated fruit of their union?) nestles pathetically on the floor.

Ernst invoked strange gods in *The Antipope*, again a representation of human and animal atavisms, and very much characteristic of the style adopted by the later fantasy artists of the Vienna school, notably Ernst Fuchs.

In later years the paintings of Max Ernst acquired a more cosmic nature and his images had a strong direction towards transcendence, which had not been present during the more tormented phases of his life.

The Marriage of Heaven and Earth, completed in 1962, finds the sky encapsulated by the folds of the yellow earth in a beautiful mandala design of great force and simplicity, and in his homage to the obscure astronomer E. Wilhelm Tempel, Ernst produced some of his most breathtaking creations. The revised edition of *Maximiliana* (1975), which saw the collaboration of Ernst with Peter Schamoni, was indicative of the continuing preoccupation Ernst had at this time with cosmic symbols of the earth, the sea, the sky and planetary constellations. An exquisite luminescent mandala was accompanied by the following poem:

The Sun
I am no black circle
I am no white square
I am no blue haze
I am heaven
I am hell
I am the bridal bed of heaven and hell
I am the spouse of all planets
The elements radiate the resplendence of my love.

This painting and others like it are especially suggestive of the Tiphareth sphere of consciousness which represents the regenerative, solar aspects of consciousness, the mandala of light in spiritual man. Tiphareth is the domain of the sun gods — Apollo, Osiris, Christ in the classical cosmologies — and provides in man an inner centering similar to the sun's position in the galaxy as the focal point of planetary rotations. In the Qabalah it is an energy source of love, new life and harmony, characteristics invariably ascribed to the great solar deities of mythology.

Ernst's vision, in a sense, transcended that of the other surrealists because while much of the effect in surreal imagery was to shock and disturb the observer — thus shaking him out of his limiting concepts of everyday reality — Ernst perhaps more than any of his peers, offered a solution of inner reconciliation.

The mythological journey of the shaman is one which takes us through the imagery of earth, and lessons comparable to those of Castaneda's Don Juan — the venture between the cracks in the worlds — are revealed by the visual jugglery of 'physical' surrealists like Magritte. Dali, Tanguy and Delvaux, in different ways, have gravitated to the lunar domain of consciousness, the world of reflections, dreams and hallucinations. Ernst remains a solitary exponent among those of the Surrealist and Dadaist persuasions, of the transcendental solar function.

We are host at the present time to a dramatic revival of the issues which underlay the whole Surrealist Movement. Just as Breton and his followers sought an extension of the limits of reality — a fully fledged incursion into the psyche — so too, as I have already indicated, we find at present an increasing preoccupation with the nature of human potential creativity and expanded forms of consciousness. Stanley Krippner has suggested that the development of interest in the healthy individual rather than the neurotic, which occurred with the birth of humanistic psychology, has had much to do with this new direction. Transpersonal psychology, with its stress on states of mind which transcend ego-oriented levels of awareness, has certainly grown out of earlier forms of growth therapy and gestalt psychology and in particular the work of Carl Rogers, Abraham Maslow and Fritz Perls.[21]

While transpersonal psychologists like Charles Tart, Montague Ullman, John Lilly and Stanislav Grof have begun to investigate mythological states of mind within the realm of consciousness research, it is abundantly clear that the surrealists were early pioneers on this inner journey.

5
The Magic of Austin Spare

Austin Spare provides us with an extraordinary instance of an artist who is also a magician and a visionary. While the Hermetic Order of the Golden Dawn — the epitome of structured ceremonial magic — was fragmenting amid schisms and dissent just prior to the onset of World War One, a unique system of magic was manifesting through Spare's visionary explorations. For Spare was probably the first modern occultist to evolve a self-contained working hypothesis about the nature of psychic energy which could be applied without all the paraphernalia of traditional rituals, grimoires and magical incantations. As we will see, Spare's system of magical sigils shows how an effort of will, when focused on the subconscious mind, can unleash the most amazing psychic material.

Spare postulated a primal and universal source of Being which he termed 'Kia' and argued that the human body, 'Zos', was an appropriate vehicle through which to manifest the spiritual and occult energies of the psyche. His technique of arousing these primal energies, an approach he named 'atavistic resurgence', involved focusing the will on magical sigils, or individualised symbols, which in effect represented instructions to the subconscious.

How exactly did Austin Spare stumble upon his special approach to magical states of consciousness? Clearly it was no accident. His magic draws on a variety of inspirational sources, including the mysteries of ancient Egypt and two unique personages: Mrs Paterson and Black Eagle.

Spare visited Egypt during World War One and was impressed by the magnetic presence of the classical gods depicted in monumental sculpture. He considered the ancient Egyptians to have been a nation of people who understood very thoroughly the complex mythology of the unconscious:

'They symbolised this knowledge in one great symbol, the Sphinx, which is pictorially man evolving from animal existence. Their numerous Gods, all partly Animal, Bird, Fish ... prove the completeness of that knowledge ... The cosmogony of their Gods is proof of their knowledge of the order of evolution, its complex processes from the one simple organism.'

For Spare, impressions from earlier incarnations and all mythic impulses could be reawakened from the unconscious. The Gods themselves could be regarded as a form of internal impetus: 'All Gods have lived [being ourselves] on earth,' he wrote, 'and when dead, their experience of Karma governs our actions in degree.' Austin Spare learnt his technique of trance activation from a witch named Mrs Paterson who claimed a psychic link with the witches of the Salem cult. In due course, Spare also began to produce automatic drawings in the trance state through the mediumship of an occult entity known as Black Eagle, who took the form of an American Indian. Spare claimed to see him several times and, in general, lived in a perceptual universe in which the everyday world and the images of trance and hallucination seemed intermingled. On one occasion, for example, while Spare was riding in a double-decker bus he found himself surrounded by imaginary passengers — an assembly of witches bound for the Sabbath!

His attraction to the ageing Mrs Paterson was paradoxical but understandable. According to Spare, she was able to transform herself in his vision from being a 'wizened old crone' to appearing quite suddenly as a ravishing siren. And for Spare, the universal woman was the central image in his mythology of the unconscious. In his definitive magical credo, *The Book of Pleasure*, he noted:

'Nor is she to be limited as any particular 'goddess' such as Astarte, Isis, Cybele, Kali, Nuit, for to limit her is to turn away from the path and to idealize a concept, which, as such, is false because incomplete, unreal because temporal.'

Spare employed a technique of ecstasy which, in his case, combined active imagination and will with the climax of sexual orgasm. Spare believed that the sigil representing the act of conscious will could be planted like a seed in the unconsciousness during such ecstasy since at this special moment the personal ego and the universal spirit blended together. 'At this moment, which is the moment of generation of the Great Wish,' wrote the magician, 'inspiration flows from the source of sex, from the primordial Goddess who 'exists at the heart of Matter

. . . inspiration is always at a *void* moment.' Several of Spare's drawings depict the Divine Maiden leading the artist into the labyrinthine
magical world. One of his most central works, *The Ascension of the
Ego from Ecstasy to Ecstasy*, shows the Goddess welcoming Spare himself, who on this occasion appropriately has wings issuing forth from
his head. Spare's 'ego', or identity, is shown merging with an earlier
animal incarnation and the two forms transcend each other in the
form of a primal skull. Spare clearly believed that he could retrace his
earlier incarnations to the universal 'Oneness of Creation', which,
within his cosmology, he termed 'Kia'. According to Kenneth Grant,
Austin Spare had derived his formula of atavistic resurgence from Mrs
Paterson:

> 'She would visualize certain animal forms and — the language of the
> subconsciousness being pictographic not verbal — each form represented
> a corresponding power in the hidden world of causes. It was necessary
> only to 'plant' an appropriate sigil in the proper manner for it to awaken
> its counterpart in the psyche. Resurging from the depths it then emerged,
> sometimes masked in that form to do the sorcerer's bidding.'[1]

Undoubtedly one of Spare's major objectives in using the trance state
was to tap energies which he believed were the source of genius. According to the artist, 'ecstasy, inspiration, intuition and dream . . .
each state taps the latent memories and presents them in the imagery
of their respective languages.' Genius itself was 'a directly resurgent
atavism' experienced during the ecstasy of the Fire Snake or Kundalinl
(i.e. sexual arousal).

Spare's Magical Cosmology

Spare's unique magical approach took several years to unfold, however, and while ancient Egyptian deities and other pagan entities abound
in his drawings, his first book seems to have been most strongly influenced by the Qabalah. This expression of Jewish Gnosticism, originally an oral tradition, has provided the main basis of contemporary
western magic, especially through its emphasis on divine names and
sacred 'words of power'. The Hermetic Order of the Golden Dawn
had distinctly Qabalistic leanings and made use of God-names in its
rituals: Egyptian deities were also frequently alluded to. Also, we know
that in 1910 Austin Spare became a member of the A∴A∴ (Argenteum
Astrum: The Silver Star), an occult group whose ritual structure Aleister
Crowley adapted from the Golden Dawn. So it comes as no real sur-

prise that as far back as the publication in February 1905 of a limited edition book *Earth: Inferno,* Spare had been developing his ideas along semi-Qabalistic patterns.

At this stage Spare tends to be dualistic: he sees things generally as either positive or negative, spiritual or materialistic, real or delusory. Human existence for him is a continuing sequence of lives during which man learns to cope with the problems and adverse situations which arise in direct relation to the ability inherent in his personality. The unenlightened, meanwhile, become bogged down in empty traditions and activities devoid of vitality. Furthermore they fail to perceive the principle 'Kia', Spare's name for the Qabalistic 'Ain Soph', which is the one Source behind all manifestation and the one Truth behind all illusions[2] Man, said Spare, ought to shed his dependency on his material security which enshrouds him in 'conventionality', and inquire instead beneath his 'mask' into his subconscious. This probing towards the macrocosm enabled man to realise his full potential. What man himself was, and what he could attain as an individual, Spare called 'Zos'[3]

His whole theory thus hinges on the relationship between Kia, the Primal Energy, and Zos, the human vehicle for receiving it. This was an inward, spiritual activity in Spare's view because he believed, as all mystics do, that the Godhead lay within. He was correspondingly dissatisfied with the world which lay without. Contemplating himself, he pondered on his own 'unreal self as humanity saw it', and came to the conclusion that he should follow the beckoning of the naked 'Primitive Woman', the Universal Mother of Nature, who could guide him pantheistically back to the Source.[4] This 'journey' which Spare describes is one within the psyche, and even in his earliest illustrated book he employs the effective device of giving symbols and ordinary depictions equal pictorial emphasis so that one is never quite sure what is 'real' in his drawings. The mystical quest is undertaken beyond 'the parapet of the subconscious' and this too is rendered as a literal circular pathway along which visionless old men dodder hopelessly looking to their candles for light, unaware of the 'Great Beyond'. People who are unable to rise above their material environment, says Spare, frequently take things on their face value; they are unable to perceive symbolic connotations. Spare shows us a depraved young man making lustful advances to the 'Universal Woman' in his failure to see beyond her enticing outward appearance. It is clearly a question of insight, for otherwise the wise, all-seeing Sophia of the

Gnosis is mistaken for the Scarlet Woman of Babylon. Spare himself did not commit this error: 'I strayed with her, into the path direct. Hail! the Jewel in the lotus!'

Mystics believe that Union with the Godhead is achieved when man is totally harmonised both within himself and externally with all things. It is the realisation that both macrocosm and microcosm are essentially the same that shatters man's ego or insularity, and leads to the Great Liberation. So we find Spare saying 'I myself am Heaven and Hell': in other words Austin Spare, in 1905 at least, was still an ego whose positive and negative qualities had not yet been reconciled or worked out. The process of harmonising these opposites in one's nature is a crucial one; Spare in his later work became highly aware of the need to overcome 'duality' in all its forms.

It is said, traditionally, that when one starts to evolve beyond the framework of the ego-centred personality, disillusionment may ensue because in the act of transcendence there is a tendency to become uprooted from humanity: correspondingly there is no longer any measure of achievement and no tangible gauge of 'progress'. Hence the term 'the black night of the soul', when one feels cut off from the world and simultaneously unable to perceive any final meaning. It is only after a great period of mental anguish that the vision of the light of God begins to dawn within the minds of those worthy to perceive it. Spare talks of this: 'The barrenness of this life but remains, yet in despair we begin to see true light. In weakness we can become strong. Revere the Kia and your mind will become tranquil.'

In the same way that the purity of aspiration is its own judge, the mystical endeavour cannot afford to be mediocre. One must be thoroughly involved and not merely a dabbler. Spare is quick to point out that the 'normal' run of things frequently involves only a halfhearted commitment: most people give only part of their time to enacting their beliefs. He quotes as his text to the illustration *The Inferno of the Normal*, two verses from *Revelations* (Ch. 3; 15, 16):

'I know thy works,
That are neither cold nor hot:
I would thou wert cold or hot.
So then because thou are lukewarm,
And neither cold not hot,
I will spew thee out of my mouth . . .

This is illustrated by a drawing of a naked[5] youth standing above the

90

parapet and drawing aside a curtain upon worldly chaos. Dishevelled bodies — the groping masses — are presented to view; these are the people who do not 'experience' but hide behind the curtain of Faith. Spare is entirely ruthless in his visual expressions, for his methods deal with self-realisation not self-trickery.

A well-known concept in occultism involves the confrontation, on an inner plane of consciousness, with the so-called 'Dweller on the Threshold'. A vile entity, an embodiment of corruption, decay, vice and sheer horror, it is none other than the accumulated self, the ego, presented to the onlooker as the anthropomorphic representation of his collected sin in incarnation. As a ghastly vision of one's 'karmic total' it has to be mentally overcome (first acknowledged, then transcended). It is not until this moment that the individual can reach beyond such degradation and realise the Divine nature behind his own appearance. And so it is that Spare comes to consider the Self as it really is: 'We realise our insignificance to the incomprehensible intellect of the Absolute Kia (the Omniscient) and find out how subcutaneous our Attainments are!' Man has to ascend from the grime of the 'Dweller on the Threshold': the self has to undergo a purgative death and be spiritually reborn as divine.

This level of attainment on the Qabalistic glyph, the 'Tree of Life', is represented by the sixth sephirah, Tiphareth, an emanation which symbolises both spiritual renewal, and also all gods who are slain and rise again (Jesus, Osiris, etc.). In portrayal, Spare shows the skulls of lions lurking behind a disconsolate woman who is tied by chains to the feet of a cross on which the legs of a nailed body are just discernible. The title is *Bodily Suffering, a resurrection of crime unpaid*; the theme is one of a Saviour figure (Christ) enduring and thus nullifying man's 'karmic debt'. This opens up the possibility that man may be rescued from the fate of a terrible death (symbolised by the skulls of lions); terrible because without the chance of rebirth or resurrection man's existence is totally and devastatingly meaningless.

Despite Austin Spare's acknowledgement of the Christ attainment, however, he remained cynical about existing religious institutions[6]. These he called 'obelisks of humanity's insignificance', projecting incapacity, the imaginations of fear, the veneer of superstition . . .' Not only was the Church too fundamentalist to transcend its own security in materialism, and its own ego; it was inherently unnecessary. For Spare believed that every human being, however 'degraded', is *essentially* Divine, although most failed to perceive it: 'I have not yet seen a man who is not God already', declares Spare provocatively. All man has to do is confront himself as he really is, and he will find God. Necessarily this involves the death of the ego, for it is the ego that insists we are distinct from other people and hence isolates us from the greater realisation of Unity. Spare therefore thought of death as a positive thing because it destroyed the pretence of personality: 'From behind, Destiny works with Death.' And death, as we have indicated, is the precursor of enlightenment: Austin Spare presents us with a Qabalistic vision:

> 'On entering at the Gates of Life,
> Lo, I behold Knowledge the Jester.
> Capsizing the Feast of Illusion,
> The drawing aside false Truth
> He shewed us all —
> The World,
> The Flesh,
> and
> The Being.
>
> This is the Alpha and Omega. . .'

In the Qabalah, Kether diagrammatically represents the first emanation of God, the act of Creation 'out of nothing'. This is the highest level spiritual man can attain[7] It is shown symbolically on the Tarot trump corresponding to the Path leading to Kether, as the Jester or Fool. The reason for this seemingly absurd representation of the sacred is as follows: Kether is the point of First-Creation and therefore total Non-Being precedes it. As a device which maintains the 'secrecy' of mystical symbols by making them outwardly nonsensical, the jester is suitably chosen, for a fool is one who knows 'nothing'. He is accordingly the wisest among all men for he has reached the highest possible state of consciousness. He has seen Kia, or negative existence.

All of this involves a relatively orthodox Western mysticism, but Spare was already developing his own individualised philosophy, devoid of all dogma or 'belief'. He was steadily eliminating — or so he hoped — the 'vices' of 'fear, faith . . . science and the like', and was preparing for the plunge into his own unknown, his inner self.

With these ideas in mind, he came to write a book entitled *The Book of Pleasure (Self Love): The Philosophy of Ecstasy*, which first appeared in 1913[8] In it were a number of important new concepts.

Sigils and Ecstasy

It is true that many occultists prior to this time had been emphasising the role of the 'will' in magical procedures. Florence Farr had outlined the need for intense mental concentration in her articles in the *Occult Review* (1908) and Aleister Crowley himself emphasised a form of mastery in 'Do what thou wilt shall be the whole of the Law', by which he meant acting in accordance with the 'higher Will' or true nature. Austin Spare adopted this view too, but only up to a point: he then moved in a different direction.

Firstly Spare dealt with the methods of concentrating the will. Since the degree of effectiveness of any action is related to a thorough understanding of the command behind the action, Spare developed a way of condensing his will so that it was more readily grasped *as a totality*. He did this by writing his 'will' (desire) in sentence form, and by combining the basic letters, without repetition, into a pattern shape or 'sign'. This could then be simplified and impressed upon the subconscious. Spare describes the process:

'Sigils are made by combining the letters of the alphabet simplified. Illustration: the word 'Woman' in sigil form is:

The idea being to obtain a simple form which can be easily visualised at will . . .'

What was to be done with the sigil once it was arrived at? And what was the significance of the sigil itself? We must first of all consider some related ideas.

As has been said before, Spare spoke of Kia as the Supreme Principle in the Universe: it was akin to a dynamic expanding Vortex of Energy, ever in a state of Becoming. Man was normally unaware of its full potential simply because he did not let it manifest in himself ('Are we not ever standing on our own volcano?'). Instead, he shut himself off by various 'insulating' devices employed by the ego. The only way in which the Energy could manifest (or be 'aroused' to use the metaphor applied to Kundalini) was by thoroughly opening oneself to it. It was when the individual was in a state of mental 'vacuity' (ultimate openness) that Kia became 'sensitive to the subtle suggestion of the sigil'. This state could be arrived at by emptying the mind of all its thought-forms in an effort to 'visualise' non-manifestation, e.g. 'blackness', 'emptiness'. In turn, this usually involved inducing meditation-leading-to-a-state-of-trance, in which the individual became oblivious of his surroundings as he focused only on the Inner Void. He would now be consciously attempting to transcend the physical, by eliminating its dominance of the senses. The contemplative state of mind, with its 'latencies', would become 'reality', rather than the earlier environment of the 'waking consciousness'.

Because we all proceed from the Godhead originally, argued Spare, it should be possible to trace back through the mind to its First Cause. Like most mystics, Spare believed in reincarnation and therefore he regarded the subconscious as the 'potential' source of all his own earlier physical embodiments or personalities, right back to the Beginning.[9] The psyche, as it were, consisted of a number of different 'layers' — The resulting impressions of successive lives, most of which were subconscious.[10] All of these were an aspect of the individual's own 'reality' (and ultimately everybody else's): in his own words, 'Know the subconscious to be an epitome of all experience and wisdom, past incarnations as men, animals, birds, vegetable life etc.: everything that has, and ever will, exist. Each being a stratum in the order of evolution. Naturally then, the lower we probe into these strata, the earlier will be the forms of life we arrive at: the last is the Almighty Simplicity.'

Spare's intention was to gain knowledge of his concealed states, through 'regression', and eventually to lose his own self or individuality 'Zos' in the indescribably ecstatic Union with Kia, whose energy he had now come to consider to be basically sexual.[11]

The dark void of the mind, emptied of thought-forms through an act of concentration, could now be penetrated by the will by employing a sigil suitable for one's purpose. According to ability, one could, in theory at least, project the sigil to all possible recesses of the subconscious and hence gain access to the entire sphere of the imagination.

In reality this was harder to achieve than the theory suggests. Obviously it depends upon a number of crucial factors:

(1) The ability to derive a suitable sigil.[12]

(2) The ability to prevent random thought-forms from unintentionally disturbing the 'black void' and thus rendering 'impure' the individual's attempt to be a pure vehicle for the energies of Kia.

(3) The ability to reach further into the subconscious by totally renouncing the worldly grip on one's aspirations. Ultimately the task involved destroying the Ego, a most unworldly activity!

This last condition was the hardest to achieve. Spare says that 'total vacuity' is 'difficult' and 'unsafe' for those 'governed by morality, complexes etc.', i.e. all the 'superstitions' and intellectual conceptions that man has surrounded himself with. Spare believed that to become totally receptive to the influx of Energy one would have to cast aside all contrived or finite rationalisations. This state of being could be achieved by any discipline nullifying the ego or intellect, but in human terms it was hard, if not virtually impossible, to arrive at. Spare therefore tried to think of various situations where the rational was minimal or absent. He tends to emphasise three such situations:

The first of these was the state of physical exhaustion. If one had a 'desire' or 'concentrated thought' in such a circumstance Spare argued, the mind would become 'worried, because of the non-fulfilment of such desire, and seek relief. By seizing this mind and living, the resultant vacuity would become sensitive to the subtle suggestion of the sigil'. In other words, by exhausting the body one made it impossible for normal mental aspirations or commands to be carried out physically. The mind was therefore 'forced' into manifesting more transcendental concepts, embodied in this case in the sigil.[13]

Sheer exhaustion can be brought about in a number of ways, but a more notorious one in mystical circles is the sexual act itself. The Tantric technique of using orgasm as the 'leaping off' point to visionary states of mind was well known at the time Spare was writing. It is probably also the basis of 'the vision of the Black Sabbath'. Aleister Crowley and Victor Neuberg, who had a homosexual relationship, employed it on a mountain in Algeria when they invoked into vision the spirit entity Choronzon.[14]

The second method lay in exploiting the mental state of extreme disappointment, experienced, say, when one lost faith in a close friend, or when a cherished ideal had been destroyed: 'When fundamental disappointment is experienced the symbol enshrining a quota of belief is destroyed. In some cases the individual is unable to survive the disillusionment. But if at such times the moment is seized upon and consciously experienced for its own sake, the vacuum attracts into itself the entire content of belief inherent in the person at the time of disappointment.' Spare is saying, in effect, that when we thoroughly lose faith in a belief or ideal, we are given the option of transcending it, and transcendence of belief leads to ecstasy, as we are drawn into the vortex of Kia.

Both these methods involve rising above a symbol, 'leaping beyond the sigil', and 'destroying an Ego-ideal', respectively, so that the organic reality of Kia is allowed full expression in the human vehicle. Kenneth Grant notes that a most important idea of Austin Spare's was to allow desires implanted by sigils (at times when the ego was negated) to 'germinate secretly and unobtrusively in the subconscious'. The desires would 'grow' in the seedbed of the mind until they became ripe and reached back down into the conscious mind. In this way one could manipulate one's own psychic 'reality'.

The desires incorporated in the sigils would eventually become moulded into the personality and the ego as such would be bypassed.

However, Austin Spare seems to have preferred a third approach, which in a sense implied the other two, and which could be used for both generalised changes in the personality and also specifics. This involved self-induced trance in which the body became rigid, ceased to function, and underwent what Spare called 'the Death Posture'. (This is similar to the second stage of Pranayama in Yoga, when after profuse perspiration the body as a whole becomes rigid. The third stage is a series of (often quite painful) spasms, described as 'jumping about like a frog', before the fourth, and rarely attained, stage of levitation.) Spare describes a preliminary exercise designed to bring the Death Posture about.

Gazing at your reflection[15] (e.g. in a tall mirror) 'till it is blurred and you know not the gazer, close your eyes and visualise. The light (always an X in curious evolutions) that is seen should be held onto, never letting go, till the effort is forgotten; this gives a feeling of immensity (which sees a small form ∞ whose limit you cannot reach.' Spare considered that this exercise should be practised daily, and its results are more fully described in his next major book which was called *The Focus of Life* (1921). But he had already alluded to the implications of the practice in an overall way.

'The Ego is swept up as a leaf in a fierce gale,' he wrote, 'In the fleetness of the indeterminable, that which is always about to happen, becomes its truth. Things that are self-evident are no longer obscure,

Austin Spare: *The Death Posture*

Austin Spare: *The Ascension of the Ego from Ecstasy to Ecstasy*

Austin Spare: *Now for Reality*

Austin Spare: *The Instant of Obsession*

Austin Spare: *Farewell to Synthesis*

Austin Spare: Untitled painting (cover for *The Search for Abraxas*, 1972)

Austin Spare: A rare trance painting from his later period

Rosaleen Norton: *Individuation*

Rosaleen Norton in her studio

Rosaleen Norton: *Timeless Worlds*

Rosaleen Norton: *The Blue-Print*

Rosaleen Norton: *Lucifer*

as by his (i.e. Spare's) own will he pleases; know this at the negation of all faith by living it, the end of the duality of consciousness'. Here Spare is alluding to the Kia dimension, which is outside Time, but which is nevertheless the central basis of all potential. Finite occurrences are latent in the unmanifest: when people 'open' themselves, certain aspects of the Kia can manifest. Pleasure for Spare was just this cosmic Realisation achieved by overcoming the dualities of the normal non-transcendent world.16 For example, he believed that he could transcend good and evil by rejecting the distinction, and he had a similar attitude to sex.

In summary his 'Death Posture' is, then, a procedure of conquering finite limitations. It seems to resemble what other writers have called 'astral projection'.

This term unfortunately conjures up all sorts of pseudo-theosophical connotations. It refers nevertheless to the hazy, variable, ever-changing realm of the subconscious with all its sense impressions and memories. Occultists believe it is possible to wander consciously in this realm, through an act of 'projection' (will) which depends firstly on imagination. The general underlying theory is that each individual is a physical body animated by consciousness, and it is this consciousness which is the sole judge of reality. Because our physical body acts in a three-dimensional way in our waking consciousness, we tend to equate reality with the 'world of the senses'.

Now if it were possible to visualise, in the imagination, a simple shape, e.g. a sphere or a cube, and by an effort of will to transfer one's consciousness by auto-suggestion to it[17] so that one felt oneself to be the sphere or cube, to be 'in' it and to 'inhabit it', reality would then appear to be of the same quality as imagination was previously. 'Astral projection' is the passing into this very dimension, the creative psyche, the 'treasurehouse of images', through an act of determination. The importance of this procedure is discussed further in another chapter. One side effect, however, is that with the extreme degree of mental detachment from everything other than the projected mental image (the cube, etc.), the body becomes numb and the individual sinks into a deep trance. He may even appear dead, hence Spare's evocative label the 'Death Posture' itself.[18]

However, the Death Posture as a concept was, for him, much more than an act of mental fantasy; it was an act involving a confrontation between the microcosm and the macrocosm, the individual Self which Spare called Zos[19] and the Kia or the 'Atmospheric I', the Infinite

Potential. It was a question of directing one's will into the cosmic memory and acquiring knowledge of earlier life-forms which were aspects of both oneself and Kia. The Death Posture provided the possibility of a link. The sigil confirmed the possibility.

A sigil, as indicated, is a visual condensation of the will. However, what we 'will' can often be based on ideas of grandeur and self-deception. Spare points out that if we imagine ourselves to be great we are not so necessarily, and all the desiring in the world can't alter the fact. Spare notes: 'Realisation is not by the mere utterance of words . . . but by the living act. . . The will, the desire, the belief, lived as inseparable, become realisation.' Hoping for something won't help us achieve it; we must 'live' it and enact it for it to become true.

In his own words Spare adds, 'Belief to be true must be organic and subconscious. The idea to be great can only become organic (i.e. 'true') at the time of vacuity and by giving it form. When conscious of the sigil form (any time but the magical) it should be repressed, a deliberate striving to forget it; by this is it active and dominates at the subconscious period; its form nourishes and allows it to become attached to the subconscious and become organic; that accomplished is its reality and realisation. The individual becomes his concept of greatness.' In summary, beliefs need to be 'organic' not theoretical in their origin; organic realities originate with Kia and lie dormant in the subconscious; we can use a sigil to embody our desire, command, or will, and it may relate to what we want to do or become; the sigil can grow in the subconscious but will lose its effect if it is consciously remembered: the sigil will eventually manifest as a 'true' aspect of the personality since it comes from within.

Spare also relates this process to the faculty of creativity: 'All geniuses have active subconsciousnesses and the less they are aware of the fact, the greater their accomplishments. The subconscious is exploited by desire reaching it.' Which implies that geniuses not born, could be made.[20] He was not the only one to have this idea.

Now the signs could embody transcendent commands affecting the whole body (Zos) or they could relate to specific senses[21] and abilities.

Kenneth Grant, who knew Spare personally, tells of a situation where Spare needed to move a heavy load of timber without assistance. A sigil was required which involved great strength, so Spare constructed a suitable sentence: 'This is my wish, to obtain the strength of a tiger.' Sigilised this word would be:

This my wish

To obtain

The strength of a Tiger

Combined as one Sigil or

Grant goes on to say: 'Spare closed his eyes for a while and visualised a picture which symbolised a wish for the strength of tigers, (i.e. the final sigil above). Almost immediately he sensed an inner response. He then felt a tremendous upsurge of energy sweep through his body. For a moment he felt like a sapling bent by the onslaught of a mighty wind. With a great effort of will, he steadied himself and directed the force to its proper object. A great calm descended and he found himself able to carry the load easily.'

Spare implied that no matter what method was used, one would arrive at 'the true sigil' for a given situation. This seems unlikely in view of the many different ways of expressing a desire. What is essentially most important, however, is that the individual is concretising his will by deriving a symbol for it that seems valid and therefore is. There is no question of whether Spare's method is 'more correct' than another: it appeared to work for him and was therefore pragmatically useful. A sigil will work for you if you believe in it.

Kenneth Grant makes it clear from his account that firstly dormant energy was awakened and then it was focused into a specialised activity. This was not always Spare's method, for in his more far-reaching 'atavistic resurgences' he allowed the influx of Kia to obsess him. His mind would become flooded with preternatural influences and there was no semblance of control.[22] Spare relates how this in itself was an act of bravery: 'Strike at the highest . . . death is failure. Go where thou fearest not. Has canst thou be great among men? *Cast thyself forth!* . . . Retrogress to the point where knowledge ceases in that Law becomes its own spontaneity and is freedom . . . This is the new atavism I would teach: Demand of God equality — Usurp!'

Thus the Death Posture, the first step, ultimately involves much more than mere transition. It involves the death of the Ego, an assault on the peak of Creation (stealing the fire from Heaven), and the utter negation of thought in supra-consciousness. But Spare at first found himself coming into contact with all sorts of forms and entities, and he came to see himself as a collection of consciousnesses, many of which were bestial and hitherto unacknowledged ('This focus "I", called consciousness, is unaware of its entire living embodiments').

Spare lets us share in his dreams, told in the third person: 'The waters became murky then muddy, and movement began.[23] Going nearer he observed a phosphorescent morass crowded with restless abortions of humanity and creatures — like struggling mudworms armless and blind: an immense swamp of dissatisfaction, a desire smashed to pieces.' This quagmire was soon none other than a vision of the 'degraded' human situation, the 'Inferno of the Normal', the terrible lethargy of inertia, that Spare himself was trying to overcome. The going was difficult, but he endeavoured to rise above it. 'He was certain he had been there before by a staircase. But now there was no easy means of access. He would have to climb whatever served. After much painful effort he managed to reach and hang on to the balustrade of the upper floor. There he noticed innumerable strange effigies and new creations of humanity. He struggled further along to obtain an easy means of ingress . . . when suddenly he observed another and more agile following him — who when reaching Aaos,[24] clutched hold of him shouting, "Where I cannot reach, thou too shalt not ascend!", their combined weight became too heavy — the balustrading collapsed and they both fell . . .'

Spare was thus dragged back from transcendence by his lower 'normal' self which resisted both the destruction of 'security' and the vision of unsuspected archetypes at higher levels of awareness. But he was determined to indulge the 'pleasure' of Union with his Higher Self, which in *The Focus of Life* he describes in increasingly sexual terms: 'Up! Up! My sexuality! and be a light unto all — that is in me.' Kia is now 'the unmodified sexuality'[25] and Spare the open vessel for its uplifting energies.

Evil and Transcendence

Direct union with the awakened diverse forms of past incarnations, beyond which lay their ultimate focus, Kia, became Spare's obsessive aim. Macrocosmically this aim constituted the Vision of the true Universal Identity; the indulgence in all the earlier shapes and outgoings of manifested experience. United in the Pleasure of Self-Recognition, this would become the Final Liberation. The world of man, of morality, science and religious dogma could no longer claim him once he had achieved macrocosmic unity with the Primal Energy. He would pass beyond experience: 'Abstinence from righteousness by total indiscrimination becomes limitlessness . . .'

There remained, however, the problem of the Devil and the nature of Evil. In *The Focus of Life*, Spare describes a terrible dream, and dreams become significant because he has previously stated that 'in future my dreams shall interpret themselves as will' (i.e. in reaction to earlier 'subconscious demands' through sigils). In this dream he visits an undertaker's apartment where he is shown his wife's dead body. The coffin meanwhile has just been constructed. Spare is 'given the choice of being burnt to death or buried alive with her! Naturally [he says] my choice was to he alone. But no such chance was to be mine . . . I was buried alive with her corpse. With their [the undertaker's assistants] combined weight forcing on the lid. I thought I was dead — for did I not hear the rushing winds? — when doubt crept into my soul. Then realisation of life dawned when I felt that cold corpse crushed against my body by the tightness of the coffin, — never have I realised such horror! With a mighty yell, my after-suspiration burst that overcrowded coffin into fragments. I arose thinking I was alone. But no, sitting by the corpse, amid the debris . . . was the Devil grinning! To be alone and half alive with the Devil is not a welcome anti-climax. . .

'Then he spoke unto me: "Coward! Where was thy courage?. . . Ah! ah! Thou hast indeed willed power. Thou or I? What medicine for the dead Gods! Thou wretched scum of Littleness — heal thy gaping wounds, thou art more fitted to pray than prey.' — Spare evidently succeeded in 'willing away' the Devil but he was obsessed with further doubts: 'Perhaps,' he says, 'I became the Devil . . .?'

We shall never know the answer of course, but the situation is reminiscent of one in which Aleister Crowley once found himself. He had reached a state of consciousness where he said of himself: 'I was in the death struggle with self. God and Satan fought for my soul . . . God conquered — now I have only one doubt left — Which of the twain was God?'[26]

Our only other clue to the workings of Spare's mind and its achievements rests in his evocative drawings, which are superbly executed and often depict in detail the 'atavistic resurgences' which Spare himself conjured up. The fact that they contain bestial elements in no way brands Spare as a diabolist because his method, as we have seen, involved 'regression' rather than the more orthodox 'evolution'.

'The Law of Evolution', says Spare, 'is retrogression of function governing progression of attainment, i.e. the more wonderful our attainments are, *the lower in the scale of Life the function that governs them.* Man is *complex,* and to progress, must become simplified.' Because more and more manifestations of Kia are appearing all the time through reincarnation, as the Source of Creation expands 'outwards', the 'true' direction is 'inwards' or 'backwards' to the First Cause.

The magnificent illustrations in *The Book of Pleasure (Self-Love),* which were drawn between 1909 and 1912, show an atavistic merging of forms. One of these, entitled *The Ascension of the Ego from Ecstasy to Ecstasy,* portrays Spare as a winged head (consciousness) rising above the Naked Primitive Woman, then merging with an ibex shape which eventually becomes a deer-skull. One plausible interpretation of this important drawing could be: Mother Nature is the door to the Greater Reality which can be found only by penetrating things as they appear. The earlier animalian (and other) incarnations can the be explored subconsciously until the Ego finds its first point of existence and then finally 'dies in the absorption within the Kia.

It is still too soon to offer any definitive observations on Austin Spare's way of thinking since it allows no immediate comparison with other schools within the Western Esoteric Tradition. It is true that a group of so-called 'Chaos magicians' now claim to be utilising Spare's sigil methods and a work recently appeared titled *Practical Sigil Magic* by Frater U∴ D∴ (Llewellyn Publications, 1990) which ostensibly extends the practical applications of Spare's trance formulations. However one has the impression that these practitioners fall far short of Spare's magical vision and have seized hold only of its pragmatic 'low magic' applications. While Frater U∴ D∴ writes that 'sigil magic is primarily success magic', Spare is exploring much wider realms than magical self-gratification: his is a unique response to the cosmos. It would be a great shame if the resurgent interest in Austin Spare was due simply to a simplification and trivilialisation of his quite outstanding contribution to magical thought.

So it is best, perhaps, to conclude with a few characteristic sayings from Austin Spare himself:

'He who subordinates animal instincts to reason quickly loses control . . . control is by leaving things to work their own salvation.'

'Only when there is no fear in any form is there realisation of identity with reality.'

'We are what we desire . . . Desire nothing and there is nothing that you shall not realise.'

'Revere the Kia and your Mind will become Tranquil.'

6

The Supernatural World of Rosaleen Norton

Rosaleen Norton has been described as Australia's best known witch but she was also one of the most remarkable painters of supernatural themes that this country has produced. Prior to her death on 5th December 1979 she lived in a shadowy basement apartment in an aging block of flats close to the El Alamein fountain in Sydney's Kings Cross. In one of her rooms she had erected a sacred altar in honour of the horned god Pan, the ancient Greek patron of pastoral life and spirit of Nature, but she kept her deepest beliefs and ideas very much to herself. A recluse from the exuberant nightlife which surrounded her, Rosaleen Norton lived in a world populated with the spirit beings and astral entities which manifested in her paintings. In recent years she decided that she didn't like people very much any more and expressed a belief in the superiority of cats, whom she felt embodied the spiritual sensitivity lacking in mankind as a whole.

There was a time when Rosaleen Norton's murals and decorative motifs spanned the walls of several popular coffee bars in Kings Cross, but these are long gone; the well known Apollyon yielded to the bypass which now takes the main flow of traffic out to the Eastern suburbs. Her heyday was in fact the late 1940s and 1950s. She was known to the public as an eccentric, bohemian witch-lady who wore flamboyant, billowing blouses and vivid bandanas, puffed on an exotic engraved cigarette holder and plucked her eyebrows so that they arched in a somewhat sinister curve. Slight in build and with long curly black hair, she always had something of a magnetic presence that made her stand out from the crowd.

Rosaleen Norton became known in the public mind as the artist whose provocative paintings of half-human, half-animal forms were even more controversial than Norman Lindsay's nude figures. She depicted naked women wrestling with reptilian elementals or flying on the backs of winged griffins, and gods who were both male and female and whose arms were like wings with claws at the extremities. These days, at a time when fantasy art has brought a vivid array of supernatural and surreal styles to record album covers, posters and T-shirts, Rosaleen Norton's paintings appear mainstream enough but in the decade after the Second World War they seemed to be an affront to human decency and ran counter to orthodox religious practice. Rosaleen had worked as a model for Norman Lindsay in the 1930s and her work resembled his in its graphic technique, which was stylised yet strongly dependent on anatomical realism.

The artist was born in 1917 in Dunedin during a violent thunder storm which she felt was a portent for her later love of the night side of life. Even when she was 3½ years of age she was fond of drawing 'nothing beasts' — animal-headed ghosts with tentacle arms — and at the age of 5 she observed an apparition of a shining dragon beside her bed. These events convinced her of the presence of the spirit world and she found herself developing religious beliefs contrary to those of her more orthodox parents. Rosaleen's father was a captain in the merchant Navy (and also a cousin of composer Vaughan Williams), her mother a 'conventional, highly emotional woman, far too absorbed in her family'.

The family migrated from New Zealand and settled in the Sydney suburb of Lindfield. Young Rosaleen lived there for the next ten years with her parents but found it increasingly difficult to relate to her mother, preferring the company of her elder sister and a favourite aunt. By the age of 14 she had decided upon the direction her life should take and was prepared to experience everything she could, 'good, bad and indifferent' and to fully express in her own way 'life and art'. A numerologist had earlier worked out her name chart and arrived at the conclusion that Rosaleen's life and work would lie well off the beaten track, a prediction which certainly came true.

Rosaleen was expelled from school under a cloud — her headmistress wrote to her mother indicating that she had 'a depraved nature which would corrupt the innocence of the other girls'. She then studied for two years at East Sydney Technical College under Rayner Hoff. During this time she became more interested in witchcraft and demonology and was well versed in the mystical writings of occultists like Dion Fortune, Aleister Crowley and Eliphas Levi long before they became fashionable in the 1960s. After leaving the college she became one of Australia's first women pavement artists, displaying her work at the bottom of Rowe Street, near the Sydney G.P.O. Her subsequent jobs included working as a newspaper cadet, designing for a toy manufacturer, assisting in a bohemian night club, waitressing, and modelling. But her work pursuits were increasingly secondary to her occult interests and in 1940 she began to experiment with self hypnosis as a means of inducing automatic drawing. She was already familiar with the trance methods of the surrealists, and especially admired the work of Salvador Dali and Yves Tanguy who, like the others of their school, had explored techniques of getting the unconscious mind to manifest its contents. Sometimes the surrealists drew rapidly so that the forms came through unimpeded by the intellect. Others experimented with drugs or documented their dream experiences with great detail, in order to develop a greater knowledge of the 'alternative reality' of the unconscious mind.

Rosaleen Norton found that she could shut off her normal consciousness by means of self hypnosis and transfer her attention to an inner plane of awareness. She notes: 'These experiments produced a number of peculiar and unexpected results . . . and culminated in a period of extra-sensory perception together with a prolonged series of symbolic visions.' She spent several years after this reading various systems of occult thought, including Buddhist and other examples of Oriental literature as well as standard works on western magic and mysticism.[1]

Her paintings became increasingly demonic although this direction had already become manifest at school when she had produced an interpretation of Saint Saens' *Danse Macabre*, complete with vampires, ghouls and werewolves. Several years later a number of her supernatural paintings were seized by police from The 49 Steps nightclub on the grounds of indecency, but the staff of *Smith's Weekly* interceded on her behalf and they were returned.

During this time, Rosaleen Norton began to activate more completely the magical forces associated with the Great God Pan, whose spirit she felt pervaded the entire earth. Her studies had taught her that the ancient Greeks regarded Pan as the lord of all things — the very totality of all elements and forms of being. He was therefore, in a very real sense, the true god of the world. Pan was a maintainer of the balance of Nature and also had at his command an invisible hierarchy of lesser spirits who could help him in his work of ruling and sustaining the earth.

The artist painted a large-scale interpretation of Pan complete with horns, pointed ears, cloven hooves and musical pipes and mounted it on the wall of her flat. She conducted magical ceremonies dressed in a tiger skin robe to honour his presence, and would often experience him as a living reality when she entered the trance state.

Meanwhile, her art continued to be a vital part of her activities and she depicted the entities encountered in visions, including devilish creatures, half animal-half human deities and various supernatural motifs. Psychiatrists were fascinated by her style and one of her paintings was bought in the early 1950s by an Adelaide bishop curious about the source of her inspiration. When English traditional artist and critic John Sackville-West arrived in Australia in 1970 he claimed that there were far too many abstract painters claiming to be artists when in fact they were really designers; he acclaimed Norman Lindsay and Rosaleen Norton as two of Australia's finest artists who were gifted in depicting detail and form.

The artist herself liked to be compared with Norman Lindsay, whom she admired and regarded, 'with Sir William Dobell, as Australia's only great artists'. She also admitted to liking and being influenced by Beardsley, Leonardo, Van Gogh and the etcher Gustav Doré but many of the world's mainstream artists, such as Picasso, Raphael and Matisse she dismissed as 'worthless'.

Rosaleen Norton's art has often been the source of considerable controversy and legal debate. She went on trial for exhibiting obscene paintings in Melbourne in August 1949 but was acquitted of all charges. Various critics had described her work as 'stark sensuality running riot', the result of 'a nightmare dipped brush' and 'as gross a shock to the average spectator as a witch's orgy' but the artist was quick to defend herself. 'Obscenity,' she countered, 'like beauty, is in the eye of the beholder. This figleaf morality expresses a very unhealthy mental attitude.'

More trouble was to come however. In September 1955, 19 year old Anna Karina Hoffmann, who was living temporarily in Victoria Street, Kings Cross, was charged by police with having unlawful means of support. She had given herself up to police because she 'couldn't stand' her lifestyle as a part-time waitress cum vagrant in Kings Cross. In court Miss Hoffmann claimed to have only £1 to her name but while evidence was being given, a number of extraordinary claims were made, some of which appeared to incriminate Rosaleen Norton.

Constable Ikin who had arrested Miss Hoffmann said she claimed to have inside information on Black Masses performed by Satanic cults and was wearing black clothing at the time because it was 'a mark of black magic'. She claimed further that Rosaleen Norton was 'the black witch of Kings Cross'.

Subsequently Anna Hoffmann denied actually taking part in a Black Mass and admitted that the connection with Rosaleen Norton was only hearsay. She was sentenced in Sydney Central Court to two months gaol and later described by Judge Holden in an appeals session as 'a menace'. However, as a result of press coverage, considerable damage had been done to Rosaleen Norton's reputation. Subsequently she had to go to great lengths to explain that the horned god Pan could not be identified with Lucifer, the god of the Satanists, and that she had never participated in a Black Mass.

Soon afterwards two Sydney newspaper reporters published a detailed eye-witness account of how they had visited a Black Mass in Kings Cross and observed a gowned witch and wizard performing a mock imitation of the Christian Mass during which a rooster was sacrificed. Public interest and newspaper coverage of alleged witchcraft activities in Kings Cross continued to percolate and Rosaleen Norton in an interview with the press claimed boldly that she had to turn prospective cult followers away in droves.

Then, quite unexpectedly on October 3, 1955, Vice Squad police raided her flat in Brougham Street and laid charges against her.

It transpired later that two men, Francis Honer and Raymond Ager, had offered the *Sun* newspaper an allegedly obscene film which purported to show evidence of a Kings Cross witchcraft cult. Two figures had been identified in the film: Rosaleen Norton and her lover, poet Gavin Greenlees with whom she had been living in a de facto relationship since 1949. Later, in ensuing court hearings, it was revealed that the films showed Norton and Greenlees garbed ceremonially in a ritual dedicated to Pan and performing 'an unnatural sexual act'. Honer had stolen the film from the artist's flat, and with Ager was attempting to sell it for £200.

The court case against Honer and Ager (who were subsequently gaoled for four months) and the extended hearings against Rosaleen Norton and Gavin Greenlees attracted extraordinary coverage in the press. Rosaleen Norton defended her religious practice of pantheism, which she described as the heathen worship of ancient Greek gods and caused raised eyebrows by appearing at the first court session flamboyantly dressed in a red skirt, black top and leopard skin shoes. Gavin Greenlees did not appear in court, though charged, because he was receiving psychiatric treatment at Sydney's Callan Park hospital. Later

Rosaleen Norton similarly took leave from the court and was found by a psychiatrist to be suffering from the aftereffects of a variety of drugs including dexedrine and methedrine, and was unable to sustain concentration. The couple were remanded on bail of £100.

Then the controversial charge of obscenity in Rosaleen Norton's art raised its ugly head again. Police officer Detective Sergeant Roy McDonald described in court how on September 9, 1955 he had visited the Kashmire Cafe in Macleay Street, Potts Point and found several of Rosaleen Norton's paintings on the wall. The owner of the cafe, David Goodman, was subsequently charged under the Obscene Publications Act with having twenty-nine of her works displayed on his premises. In the Special Court, Mr. Dash S.M. described the paintings, which included such works as *Black Magic, Beezlebub and Belphagor* as being lewd, lustful and erotic' and fined Goodman £5 plus costs for displaying paintings which could attract the curious and avid. The court hearings dragged on for almost two years and finally, in Central Court, Norton and Greenlees were convicted and fined £25 each for having assisted an unknown photographer in making obscene pictures in June 1955.

Understandably after these unfortunate and extended court hearings which in every way impinged upon her personal though unorthodox mystical beliefs, Rosaleen Norton began to withdraw from the public eye. Although she still gave intermittent interviews to journalists and appeared occasionally on radio and television, her main interest was to be able to continue to paint, and to obtain enough commissions for a steady income.

The lurid media publicity surrounding her work has tended to override the essential importance of both her magical vision and the techniques of trance which she used to conjure the supernatural entities involved. For example, many occultists have applied the theories of Swiss psychoanalyst Carl Jung to relate magical experiences to the forces of the so-called 'Collective Unconscious'. Jung took the view that at a deep layer of the psyche lay a rich and varied source of archetypal images which were the very basis of religion and mystical expression, irrespective of the culture or society involved. Other occultists reject this view, claiming instead that the gods live apart from the minds of men and are not merely projected 'thought-forms'. Rosaleen Norton agreed with the latter perspective. In an interview given the year before her death she explained that she believed it to be very egotistical and self-centred to place man on a pedestal in creation. For her the gods existed in their own right. She knew Hecate, Lucifer and Pan, not as extensions of her own consciousness, but as beings who would grace her with their presence if it pleased *them*, and not subject to her will. She believed that she had discovered certain of the qualities of these gods in her own temperament and that this was a natural catalyst which made their invocation much easier and more effective. She went to be with them on the astral planes, and on different occasions it could be said that they showed different aspects or facets of their own magical potency.

Rosaleen Norton regarded Lucifer not as 'evil' so much as man's adversary. He bound and limited man when it appeared that he was growing too big for his boots. He tried to trick man, not with malicious intent, so much as by exposing the limitations of the ego and man's pride in his own existence. She regarded Pan as a very significant deity for the present day, a force in the universe which protects and conserves the natural beauty and resources of the environment. Pan is alive and well in the anti-pollution lobbies and among the Friends of the Earth!

Hecate on the other hand she felt to be more imposing, a frightening shadowy goddess flanked by cohorts of ghouls and night-forms, a dealer in death and a purveyor of curses. But there was a magical bond to be found here too. Rosaleen Norton regarded magic and witchcraft as her protection and inspiration in a fairly hostile, ungenerous world. Her own witchcraft hardly brought her abundance. She lived simply, with few possessions and certainly without wealth. If she ever cursed people with 'witch current' it was as a means of redressing the balance of events, a legitimate use of the magical art.

Rosaleen's paintings, as already mentioned, show a certain similarity of style to those of Norman Lindsay. But whereas for Lindsay, the world of supernature could only offer themes, for Rosaleen Norton it was an ongoing reality. This is very much reflected in her work. There are fire elementals, ablaze with light; devils with dual banks of eyes, indicative of their different planes of perception; cats with magical awareness; horned beings with sensual cheeks and a strange eerie light playing on their brow. Her art was the result of the magical encounter. Energies filtered through her, she said, as if she were a funnel. She transmitted the current. If the gods were alive in her, her artistic medium allowed them to manifest, in degrees, upon her canvas.

Rosaleen Norton always denied that she portrayed the totality of the god. She could depict only those qualities the god chose to show.

The gods existed in their own right, on a plane removed from man's everyday consciousness. The role of the magician was to enlarge his consciousness to take in all these possibilities, to walk in his world knowing it to be populated by all manner of beings and entities.

In certain of Rosaleen's paintings we find creatures which are half human and half animal. These in many ways are her most convincing magical works. For Rosaleen Norton these creatures were in no way degraded beings. If she depicted warlike force as an anthropomorphic hawk, it was because within the domain of animals and birds the hawk very admirably embodied the symbolism of destructiveness and aggression. When portraying Jupiter it was fitting that the king should have lion's legs and paws because the lion was a motif of royalty, of dominance and command. Several illustrations of this type were reproduced in a volume of the artist's drawings which was published in 1952 in a limited edition of one thousand copies. The drawings were in black and white and accompanied a series of poems by Gavin Greenlees.[2]

Greenlees, who died in 1983, was a modest and quietly spoken man for whom the magical view of the world was simultaneously a visionary and poetic expression. Like Yeats, he had been drawn to the Tarot as a series of mystical images; he authored a series of Tarot poems, now lost, which Rosaleen Norton considered to have been among his best work.

In the published edition, Rosaleen Norton's artwork appeared in the context of a series of magical statements, both in terms of Greenlees' poetry, but also as an adjunct to the names of major supernatural forces. It was documented with magical sources that did not become well known until the growth of interest in occultism during the 1960s.

In an introduction to the book, publisher Walter Glover noted the parallels in Rosaleen Norton's art and certain of the Surrealists, and also pointed out that her paintings embody what he called 'a vision of the night'. Rosaleen Norton had spontaneous magical experiences long before becoming acquainted with the means of structuring them through the terminology of demonology and witchcraft.

She herself always regarded art as a medium for expressing an alternate and much more impressive reality than the dimension of normality obfuscated by human beings. In an early journal entry she wrote:

> There are senses, art forms, activities and states of consciousness that have no parallel in human experience ... an overwhelming deluge of both Universal and Self Knowledge presented (often in an allegorical

form) from every conceivable aspect . . . metaphysical, mathematical, scientific, symbolic . . . These comprise a bewildering array of experiences each complete in itself yet bearing an interblending and significant relationship to every other facet.

One such experience could be compared with simultaneously watching and taking part in a play in which all art forms, such as music, drama, ceremonial ritual, shape, sound and pattern, blended into one . . .

Rosaleen's art was considerably varied. Her paintings and drawings ranged from satirical, but essentially whimsical, parodies on church figures, to Boschean whirlpools of energy forms interacting with each other, and representations of great supernatural deities.

Rosaleen's representation of Mars — the warlike entity — for example, shows a powerful human male torso with the winged head of a hawk. The god has a scorpion's tail and clawed feet and very much embodies a sense of power and aggression. He holds a sphere in his right hand which could almost be the puny globe of Earth, under his influence.

Her portrait of Jupiter shows a proud potentate with a resplendent light issuing from his forehead, and a dark, majestic beard lapping down on to his chest. His legs and tail are leonine, and he carries in his right hand the mace of authority.

In both of these pictures, Rosaleen Norton depicts her deities as an animal-human fusion. For her, animals characterise a dignity that man has lost. She is especially fond of cats because of their 'psychic qualities', and the lion therefore becomes an appropriate symbolic aspect of one of the major rulers of the magical universe.

Rosaleen felt that the animal kingdom had retained its integrity to a far greater extent than the human. She was one with animals, for whom she felt a natural empathy. Many human beings, however, she despised for their narrow world-view. Cats, by contrast, operated in waking consciousness and on the astral plane simultaneously.

She recalled what she felt may have been a previous incarnation. She lived in a past century in a rickety wooden house in a field of yellow grass near Beachy Head in Sussex. There were animals — cows, horses and so on — and she was a poltergeist. She remembered understanding the techniques by which poltergeists made objects move. And yet when 'real' people came near her house they were offended and frightened by her presence. They could not relate to her poltergeist condition, and she in turn found herself attacking them out of contempt. The animals however were no trouble at all. They regarded her as another cohabitant, as part of the 'natural order'.

Her love of animals and her antipathy towards much of what the human race has come to represent of course influenced her magical conceptions. And yet she acknowledged duelling factions within the animal kingdom as representing important themes of 'polarity'.

The hawk, for example, she saw as a natural predator, a fitting representation of the Martian archetype. Her preference for animals was thus clearly not an escape into the non-human. On the contrary the animal kingdom contained a range of activities and functions from which mankind had much to learn.

The necessity for a sense of balance shows itself well in another of her pictures, *Esoteric Study*. An angry demon leers across from the realm of chaos counterbalanced by a diamond shape of white radiance on the other side. The scales are issuing out of the cosmic egg and the superimposition of the magician's face on the scales themselves suggests that the artist is the vehicle through which all the tides of energy flow, asserting their polarities of balance accordingly.

Gavin Greenlees' accompanying poem begins:

Out of herself, the Earth created by her own Guardian faces,
And using the rule they gave her, out of herself
She made creatures to serve her, — animals, poems,
Forgotten beings, men, women . . . Out of herself
She made the grandeur aid its faith, healthy or faded . . .[3]

One of Rosaleen Norton's most impressive portraits is titled *Individuation*. She has denied a direct influence from the Tarot, regarding it more as an intuitive source than as a series of meditative doorways to inner states. Nevertheless, in several respects we find here a parallel with the Tarot card *Temperance*. The figure depicted is a fusion of the animal, the human and the divine:

I speak the birth,
I speak the beginning of presence
I am inauguration, I am a greeting between friends
One flower, one animal, one phrase,
One illusion, one discovering in one world![4]

The figure stands astride the Zodiac drawn down into a mountain of forms, yet rising transcendent above them. The drawing follows

Panic which closely resembles *The Tower*, the card in the Tarot which provides a symbolic warning of the forceful energy levels of high states of being.

Rosaleen Norton's tower is exceptionally organic and phallic, again indicative of the fertility aspect of witchcraft. It is surmounted by the Horned God — horns symbolising for her the dual polarities of magical energy. A cascade of liquid energy courses around the column, and in the bottom of her picture we notice a hand causing a wave of astral forms.

As we have said, Rosaleen Norton's expression of her magical universe did not always attract a receptive audience. During the period when obscenity accusations were levelled at her work, a large part of the limited edition was destroyed by customs police and in the present day Rosaleen Norton's art has been neglected and forgotten. The public recalls her status as a witch, with its unbecoming connotations, but has forgotten her significance as a magical artist.

This is undoubtedly a misconception. Rosaleen Norton was clearly no mere 'witch'. She lived in a world of magical beings and astral entities who manifested in various degrees in her remarkable paintings. There is no question that Rosaleen Norton was one of the forerunners of contemporary occult exploration.

Part Two

EXPLORING THE NEW CONSCIOUSNESS

Beyond the New Age: From Holistic Health to Sacred Psychology

On the surface, certainly at first glance, the New Age can appear very superficial. It is also a phenomenon that is easy to parody. If one can believe the popular media image, a New Ager is a person who believes in astrology, channelling, reincarnation and telepathic bonds with dolphins, eats organically grown fruits and cereals, is obsessed with the healing power of crystals, casts a daily horoscope or consults the *I Ching*, talks to trees, and has a personal philosophy that is so optimistic that it makes naivety into an artform. It has not helped that in a consumerist society where anything in demand can be marketed that assuaging spiritual thirst has itself become a commodity. And so we find in our midst a vast array of personal and metaphysical 'transformation' courses — many of them marketed for excessively high fees. Some might come with the tag, for example, that money is simply 'a unit for power and energy' and that 'prosperity consciousness' is potentially available to us all if we can but 'take the responsibility' to recognise our own self-worth. On this level the New Age appears glossy, yuppie, materialistic and potentially elitist, for those able to graduate to these new levels of self-realisation might then almost feel themselves to be a distinct category of more 'evolved' human beings.

As with all parodies, of course, there is an element of truth in all of this. However, to assume that the New Age is. on this level only — a marketplace populated mainly by psychic channellers and unscrupulous merchandisers — is to miss the point that at a deeper level a much more important process of social and spiritual change seems to be under way. Some New Agers and members of the Human Potential Movement have called this change a 'paradigm shift' and it certainly does involve a realignment of personal perspectives and spiritual allegiances. It is a broad-based movement which at times appears tire-lessly eclectic and is thus difficult to define succinctly. There are, nev-ertheless, distinctive themes and attitudes which characterise it as an approach to life: the New Age is not entirely nebulous.

If one had to begin by defining the core characteristics of New Age thought one would surely talk in terms of a holistic approach to life and an emphasis on connectedness. This is a very different type of world-view from that, say, of the Existentialists, who maintained that we each live in our own distinct universe where our own existence is the only thing we can be sure of. According to this philosophy, hu-mans are essentially isolated from each other, life has no intrinsic meaning or purpose and there is ultimately no code of good and evil. While Existentialist philosophers like Jean-Paul Sartre believed that our individual existence separates us from other people and from the world at large, the New Age view is that everything is interconnected. Life is perceived as a type of flux in which all people on the planet are in varying degrees of interdependence, our future as fellow travellers being globally determined by our capacity to share a common des-tiny. It is also a world-view which proposes a fusion of the materialis-tic and the spiritual, the tangible and the intangible, so that one does not define 'humanness' simply in physical terms but also in a language which acknowledges the metaphysical and transcendent. Thus, in terms of health, one's wellbeing is not characterised in a reductionist way by the absence of disease entities but in terms of the integration of physi-cal, mental and spiritual qualities — a perspective popularly known as 'holistic health' — and environmental awareness may similarly be de-fined in terms of recognising the 'sanctity' of Nature or the 'sacred-ness' of the planet.

On this level, the New Age certainly takes a broader rather than a narrower perspective of life — sometimes to the point where interconnectedness (say, between man and dolphin or with channelled discarnate sages) may acquire more than a hint of irrationality. How-ever the New Age is consciously 'open' in its preferences and champi-ons viewpoints in which experiences of the heart are valued every bit as much as perspectives derived from logic and intellect.

Astronaut Edgar Mitchell embodied the global frameworks of the New Age when he described that it was like to view the Earth from space. As he watched the planet floating in space from his special van-tage point in Apollo XIV he felt a profoundly new orientation. 'I had some life-changing insights,' he recalled later. 'In psychological terms you might say I had a peak spiritual experience. It was seeing from a different perspective and rethinking everything I knew from this different way of looking. It was an experience of identification — of being one with the universe and sensing the unity of all things.'

So, in this sense, a dominant characteristic of New Age thought is extending the capacities of one's vision. This may lead in turn to new modalities of self-awareness (meditation and visualisation techniques, float tanks, rebirthing, relationships training), support for business practices which are ethically and ecologically sound and which are oriented towards outcomes that eliminate conflict (the so-called 'win-win' philosophy), greater environmental awareness (recognition that one can make responsible decisions relating to environment-friendly products, recycling of waste, conservation of energy and the rethinking of an exploitive attitude towards Nature's resources) and a more broadly based expression of spirituality (for example, a capacity to learn not simply from the religious faith one grew up with, but from all of the great spiritual teachings and traditions). To this extent, as well known New Age author Marilyn Ferguson has put it, the emphasis is on 'an expanded view of the human condition, forcing us to rethink the nature of our minds, bodies and social problems.' Let us now consider some of the major themes of the New Age:

Utopian Optimism
As an overall philosophy, New Age thinking has as its overriding aim the wish to create a better society — one which is more just, where power resides more with individuals than with hierarchies and institutions (and is thus guided to a larger extent by personal intuition and insight) and where national boundaries and regional instincts are less important than a sense of global awareness and international co-operation. As David Spangler, co-founder of the Findhorn Community, has written:

> 'The New Age has . . . everything to do with the imagination to see our world in new ways that can empower us towards compassion, transformative activities and attitudes.'[2]

To this extent the New Age continues the vision of the New England Transcendentalists like Ralph Waldo Emerson, Henry David Thoreau, Amos Alcott and James Freeman Clarke. Precursors of Spiritualism, Theosophy and contemporary approaches to Zen Buddhism — all of which continue as elements in the New Age. The Transcendentalists sought spiritual ways of living in an America which, as Robert Ellwood has written, was 'intoxicated with the ideas of change, expansion and a brighter tomorrow.' Well versed in Eastern mystical philosophy, they sought an idyllic lifestyle at such locations as Walden and the communal Brook Farm. The following words come from Thoreau:

'In the morning (at Walden Pond) I bathe my intellect in the stupendous and cosmogonal philosophy of the Bhagvat Geeta, since whose composition years of the gods have elapsed and in comparison with which our modern world and its literature seem puny and trivial . . . The pure Walden water is mingled with the sacred water of the Ganges.'

The Transcendentalists felt that amidst the increasing complexities of life, American society was ignoring its spiritual roots and losing touch with Nature and Soul. The New Age similarly endeavours to see the world through new eyes — guided by an intent towards profound and enduring social transformation. For its devotees, the New Age will hopefully herald in a new era of social harmony and holistic living, in accord with Nature.

Holistic Health and Feelings of Connectedness

The New Age perspective emphasises a sense of connectedness with others, with Nature and — by extension — with the planet. Since the early days of the Human Potential Movement in the 1960s and 1970s much more attention has been given, in alternative health circles, to exploring the nature of relationships through deep personal inquiry group encounter work and techniques of conflict resolution. Following Maslow's emphasis on the healthy 'self-actualised' person as a social role model, the encounter therapies, for example, sought to develop processes whereby people could learn to rediscover a sense of pleasure, joy and self-fulfilment in their lives — basic aspects of being human that all too often have been undermined by the intense urban pressures we all endure. The encounter therapy work pioneered by such figures as Carl Rogers and Will Schutz has led to a wide range of interpersonal health modalities which emphasise positive relations with others, a sensitivity towards human differences, the fostering of mutual understanding and, in some instances, the development of support groups aimed at assisting people suffering from life-threatening diseases like cancer and AIDS.

Underlying these activities is a basically 'holistic' way of viewing human health. The term 'holism' was first used in modern times in

1928 by the philosopher Jan Smuts in his book *Holism and Evolution* but the concept is much older than this. *Holos* is the ancient Greek word for 'whole' and from it we derive our English expressions 'holy', 'whole', 'health' and even the greeting 'hello'. Plato was an early advocate of the holistic approach to wellbeing as the following quotation makes clear:

> 'The cure of the part should not be attempted without treatment of the whole. No attempts should be made to cure the body without the soul, and if the head and body are to be healthy you must begin by curing the mind, for this is the great error of our day in the treatment of the human body, that physicians first separate the soul from the body.'

Fortunately there are doctors and healthcare professionals who are beginning to apply the Platonic philosophy in the modern context. In *Dimensions of Humanistic Medicine*, a modern treatise on holistic medicine, the authors make an appeal for a return to a broader vision of mankind:

> 'A person is more than his body. Every human being is a holistic, interdependent relationship of body, emotions, mind and spirit. The clinical process which causes the patient to consult the medical profession is best understood as this whole and dynamic relationship. The maintenance of continued health depends on harmony of this whole.'

It may be worthwhile at this point to briefly summarise the principal characteristics of holistic health since many of these themes are an integral part of New Age thought as well:

- Health is seen as a positive and natural state and is conceived in terms of the whole being of the person, not in terms of rectifying a particular isolated symptom.

- The frame of reference is much broader than the purely physical. It encompasses the mental and emotional aspects of health and also such areas as spiritual values, the search for personal meaning, and the integrative nature of religious beliefs. Stress, for example, is considered to be a state of imbalance between parts of the organism in relation to the whole.

- The focus is more on prevention than cure. This brings with it an emphasis on such self-help factors as sensible nutrition, exercise and personal involvement in preventing the onset of disease. Where cures are required, treatments will not be simply for symptoms but for balance, integration and total well-being.

- The person is encouraged to take responsibility for his state of health and to be as self-reliant as possible. The emphasis is on the positive promotion of health and the prevention of disease.

- Illness may be perceived as providing the opportunity for personal growth and self-discovery. One learns to question why a condition of imbalance has arisen and to seek ways of rectifying personal deficiencies which may have contributed to such disease states. This is particularly true in the case of holistic treatments for cancer, where emotional or lifestyle imbalances are isolated as a cause of stress, contributing to breakdowns in the immune system and the outbreak of tumours. Similarly, nutritional factors such as excessive intake of saturated fats, may be perceived as contributing to coronary heart disease and new and more balanced lifestyle adopted as a consequence.

- Respect is paid to ancient and traditional systems of healthcare like acupuncture, herbalism, ayurvedic medicine and yoga as well as to the advances of modern scientific medicine. The earlier modalities are seen as having value as 'complementary' styles of medicine and as being useful adjuncts to modern science. Holistic therapists have no inherent problem in utilising systems not fully understood within the western scientific paradigm.

- The patient is encouraged not to become dependent on the doctor but to take increasing control of his own situation.

- The emphasis is placed on the remarkable capacity of the human organism to rectify imbalance and engage in a self-healing process. 'Natural modalities' stimulate healing processes to occur from within the organism wherever possible, rather than relying on an external agent that is 'alien'. This means that healing should be as nonintrusive as possible and should not involve potentially toxic drugs or any other 'unnatural' agents.

The holistic approach to health is a comparatively recent development in modern medicine and has emerged largely as a response to stress as an underlying cause of disease.

One of the leading advocates of holistic lifestyles is Dr Kenneth Pelletier of the University of California School of Medicine in San Francisco. Dr Pelletier argues in his book *Mind as Healer, Mind as Slayer* that stress is necessary for most forms of positive activity but that in western society this has become excessive and self-destructive.

The models of behaviour most admired in our society now involve high stress levels — focusing on personal ambition, goal orientation and financial prosperity — and this means that we all have to learn how to cope with stress more efficiently. Part of the approach in holistic counselling is thus to try to isolate the stressors in one's lifestyle — that is to say, specific causes of stress — and eliminate them systematically.

This in turn has led many New Agers to explore a range of experiential approaches to stress-reduction, including a variety of meditation procedures (TM, Siddha Yoga, Raja Yoga, Zen etc.) and relaxation exercises accompanied by visualisation and ambient music. For many, too, this pursuit of meditative techniques has led also to the exploration of other spiritual disciplines and traditions. For some New Agers, formal Christianity has remained too doctrinal and insufficiently 'experiential': Eastern mystical religions like Hinduism and Buddhism, which offer a number of practical approaches for stilling the mind and allowing oneself to open to the inner spirit, have become popular as substitute spiritual paths.

The Sacred Earth

New Agers have long admired the apparently intuitive capacity of many native peoples to live harmoniously with Nature. This type of feeling is epitomised by the following Navajo song:

The thoughts of the earth are my thoughts.
The voice of the earth is my voice.
All that belongs to the earth belongs to me.
All that surrounds the earth surrounds me.
It is lovely indeed; it is lovely indeed.

This type of holistic consciousness is also found in the account of the Oglala Sioux shaman, Black Elk, who stood on the summit of Harney Peak and experienced a vision of the universe uplifted by a profound sense of harmony and balance:

'. . . I was standing on the highest mountain of them all, and round about beneath me was the whole hoop of the world and while I stood there I saw more than I can tell and I understood more than I saw, for I was seeing in a sacred manner the shapes of things in the spirit, and the shape of all shapes as they must live together like one being. And I saw that the sacred hoop of my people was one of many hoops that made one circle, wide as daylight and as starlight, and in the centre grew one mighty flowering tree to shelter all the children of one mother and one father. And I saw that it was holy.'

Such feelings of perceiving the earth and one's relationship with it as sacred are, of course, intrinsic to the belief systems of many native cultures. For the Australian Aborigines the land has sacred significance because it was bequeathed to them through the primordial events of the Dreamtime. Aboriginal ceremonies are a symbolic expression of this sacred bond, enabling the cycles of life to continue. As James Cowan writes in *Mysteries of the Dreaming*:

'Aborigines had no conception of themselves as the "crown" of God's creation in the way that world religions often deify man. Life *per se* was a web of interactive particles, of which mankind and nature were co-equal partners. Therefore the role of mankind in the drama of life was to re-create through ritual and ceremony the eternal moment of the Dreaming . . . Tribal land then became a living entity insofar as it contributed to the overall sustenance of life.'

The primal idea of a holistic bond with Nature has become part of New Age mythology as well, and has been substantially influenced by the idea that the planet is itself a living system — a concept reinforced by the so-called 'Gaia Hypothesis'.

Gaia was the ancient Greek 'Earth Mother' and in New Age belief is one of the many personifications of Mother Nature — herself an archetype of renewal and abundance. However, the Gaia Hypothesis is not only a spiritual metaphor but also a scientific proposition. It was put forward by the British chemist Dr James Lovelock, a former consultant to the California Institute of Technology, who at one time worked on the scientific investigation of life on Mars.

While Lovelock concluded on the basis of his study of the relatively static Martian atmosphere that no life existed on that planet, he became intrigued by the dynamics of Earth's atmosphere. He found, for example, that Earth's atmosphere differed greatly from the levels anticipated by physical chemistry. The concentration of atmospheric oxygen is around 21 per cent, and yet in theory since oxygen is a very reactive gas, it should be almost completely absorbed, thus resulting in an atmospheric level close to zero. Lovelock was also fascinated by the fact that Earth's atmosphere was able to retain a composition suitable for the continuation of life on the planet. His conclusion was that the Earth's atmosphere was affected by a wide range of living processes on the Earth itself, all of which helped maintain the atmosphere and the surface temperature: in short that the Earth was a type of organically interrelated 'whole'. Gaia became Lovelock's metaphor for Earth's total biosystem, including the atmosphere, oceans and landforms, and all of Earth's plants, animals and fungi. This biosystem contributed to a state of homeostasis appropriate for the conditions of life.

Lovelock collected an extensive body of evidence for planetary homeostasis and presented it in his book *Gaia: a New Look at Life on Earth*. Included were details of such comparatively 'constant' factors as Earth's surface temperature (which seems to have remained within a tolerable range for many millions of years, enabling life to continue); the salt content of the oceans (around 3.4%); the oxygen concentration in the atmosphere (21%) the amount of atmospheric ammonia (allowing rain and soil to have the right degree of acidity to support life) and the continued existence of the ozone layer in the upper atmosphere.

Gaia, as Peter Russell writes in *The Awakening Earth*, thus 'appears to be a self-regulating, self-sustaining system, continually adjusting its chemical, physical and biological processes in order to maintain the optimum conditions for life and its continued evolution.'[8] While Lovelock himself has resisted identifying the biosphere as a single living organism, the Gaia Hypothesis has nevertheless become a powerful metaphor for global environmental awareness. In New Age thinking the Earth itself is then seen as having consciousness — it is alive. This idea, of course, is also reflected in the belief systems of animistic native cultures. For the American Indians the planet is the Mother of all living beings animals, plants, rocks and human beings are all interrelated. For Native American teachers like Sun Bear — himself a prominent figure in New Age circles — this holistic awareness of the environment has a healing, transformative implication:

'If you teach people to find a better balance within themselves, how to be stronger, centre their life, and go forward with a good balance upon the Earth Mother, then that is a healing. You take away all the little pains when you teach people to become self-reliant . . . When people have centred themselves, they know that they can draw power from the universe.'

Ralph Metzner, an influential figure in the Human Potential Movement, contrasts such traditional responses to Nature with the sort of ethic that modern western civilisation has developed in its relationship with the environment:

'The metaphor of man against Nature, at war with Nature and the elements, is one that many people have formulated. It has a kind of religious world-view rationale in certain aspects of the Christian technological civilisation of Europe and North America. It represents the shadow side of our obsession with individual separateness and power. At the same time there are concepts and attitudes of the mystics, or shamanic cultures and contemporary formulations of ecologically holistic world-views that promise a way out of the self-created dilemmas of humankind.'

Self-Transformation

It is a truism in the New Age that one should transform oneself before endeavouring to transform others. While at times this might appear to be an extremely self-centred attitude, the personal focus on one's own transformation represents only the first step in the journey. The task, initially, is to explore the facets of one's own individuality, to integrate these aspects as far as one is able, and then to develop this integrative state of awareness in one's relationships with others, and within the environment. The field of self-awareness thus extends outwards in circles of ever-increasing range, rather like the ripples created by a stone when it is thrown into a pond.

If we consider the Holistic Health model mentioned earlier, it is clear that the process of individual integration needs to occur on a number of levels — physical, mental, emotional and spiritual. A diverse range of 'alternative' modalities — some admittedly more authentic than others — has sprung up to cater for this need. Underlying all these modalities, however, is a common theme of self-transformation and the credo that if we all were to transform ourselves and raise our culture to 'the next phase of human evolution' then the world would surely be a much better place in which to live.

Numerous books have appeared during the last twenty years covering the various holistic modalities explored and embraced by the New Age. Here is a brief summary of some of the main New Age therapies and the core concepts behind them.

Body: The collective term for physical therapies is 'bodywork' and this includes a wide range of modalities for freeing muscle spasms, correcting poor posture and maximising efficient body use. It also includes cathartic techniques which release emotional trauma expressed in the musculature of the body. Bodywork techniques include the many different forms of massage and physical yoga as well as the Alexander Technique, chiropractic, osteopathy, shiatsu, Reichian Therapy, Rolfing, Feldenkrais Awareness Through Movement, deep tissue muscle therapy, rebirthing and Shintaido.

One of the uniting concepts in bodywork is the idea of a 'lifeforce' flowing through the body. Known in China as *chi* in Japan as *ki*, and in Reichian Therapy as 'orgone energy', it is thought to flow unimpeded through the human organism when the latter is in a state of harmony and integration.

Mind: New Age approaches to the mind may be found on several different levels. In the motivational area, which focuses very much on the individual and his or her latent potential, there are numerous variations on the theme of mental development and 'creative visualisation', most of which have as their end-goal a sense of individual self-reliance and the creation of wealth, happiness and 'prosperity'. Examples include Silva Mind Control, est, Forum, Own Your Life, Money and You and a number of self-hypnosis programmes. Also within this category are modalities whose main purpose is the reduction of stress. These include Transcendental Meditation (TM) and the use of ambient New Age music composed by such figures as Steven Halpern, Steve Roach, Aeoliah and David Sun as an aid to relaxation and visualisation'. The school of thought known as Psychosynthesis, developed by the Italian psychiatrist Dr Roberto Assagioli (1888-1974), also includes a number of integrative visualisation approaches aimed at developing awareness of both the will and the 'higher self'.

Emotions: When New Agers wish to treat their emotions they generally turn to the so-called Bach Flower Remedies. These remedies were discovered by Dr Edward Bach (1880-1936), a Harley Street physician who became convinced that medicine should not be preoccupied with disease symptoms so much as the mental conditions underlying them. In 1930 Bach abandoned his medical practice and went to live in the countryside. He believed that he would be able to identify medicinal healing agents in the wild flowers growing in the fields and meadows for, as he wrote in his book *Heal Thyself*: 'Among the types of remedies that will be used will be those obtained from the most beautiful plants and herbs to be found in the pharmacy of Nature.'

Over a seven-year period Dr Bach identified 38 flowers which appeared to him to have healing qualities and which he believed could be used to treat emotional afflictions. These included rock rose and cherry plum 'for fear'; cerato and scleranthus 'for uncertainty'; water violet and heather 'for loneliness' and sweet chestnut and crab apple 'for despondency or despair'.

More recently the Australian naturopath Ian White has identified a number of 'Australian bush essences' which he believes represent native counterparts to Bach's English wildflower remedies. These include dog rose 'for fear or shyness', five corners 'for low self-esteem', sun dew 'for vagueness', black-eyed Susan 'for impatience', slender rice flower 'for jealousy' and waratah 'for deep despair'.[11]

Spirit: As one would perhaps expect, it is in the area of New Age approaches to the Spirit that one finds the most questionable concepts and practices. It goes without saying that New Age spiritual modalities range extensively in their degree of authenticity and commerciality.

One of the most controversial practices of this sort is channelling — an activity associated with New Age personalities like Shirley MacLaine, J. Z. Knight and the late Jane Roberts (the last two being channellers of Ramtha and Seth respectively). Channelling is really a new name for spiritualism or mediumism. Here the psychic is believed to act as a channel for communications from the spirit-world. Channellers claim to obtain information which can in turn be offered to their clients as advice for managing their day-to-day affairs. Sometimes, however, channelled entities provide messages which purport to have greater spiritual significance. In November 1987, J. Z. Knight channelled these thoughts from Ramtha: 'God is both male and female and yet neither. That which lives in the woman is as powerful and divine as that which lives in the man'. . .'God is the essence, it permeates your entirety'. . .'Within you lies the ability for profound knowingness. Like the Mother Earth, a wisdom, a courage, a dignity to evolve'. . .[12]

While these pronouncements may seem comparatively uncontroversial, Ramtha also spoke of a huge wave which would soon flood Sydney, that people should hoard their gold supplies, and that there would be further stock exchange collapses and attempts by governments to reduce citizens' financial free will. Ramtha, in fact, has become something of an international personality in his own right, manifesting his distinctly masculine voice through the very feminine form of J. Z. Knight on such television programmes as The Merv Griffin Show in the United States, and at numerous seminars around the world.

Another New Age practice which has attracted widespread media ridicule and which has come to personify the more credulous aspects of the New Age, is the idea of healing with crystals. In an article in the 'alternative' publication *Southern Crossings* (August 1985) Lynette Mayblom described how 'crystals have wonderful uses in the area of personal healing but they can also be used on a greater scale for world healing. Crystals can be used to focus love and light on important buildings and places, to construct triangles of light in the planet's etheric body, to assist the growth of plants and to protect and purify your home.' Mayblom went on to relate how crystals could also be used in spiritual meditation: 'Triangles of light can be set up between three people by meditating daily at the same time with crystals. These people can visualise light flowing from their third eyes to the other two, creating a triangle of light and visualising the encompassed area filled with light. Distance is of no consequence . . .'[13]

It needs to be emphasised that crystals are by no means a cheap commodity and only the more affluent New Agers can afford crystals of any size. New Age enthusiast Bianca Pace told journalist Mark Chipperfield that she marketed quartz crystals for between $600 and $4000 each, and that her crystals had 'the power to cure diseases and transmit human and cosmic thoughts'. Crystals, she maintained, 'are part of the energy grid of the planet'.[14]

Some New Agers attend regular therapy sessions where their *chakras* (spiritual centres in the body) are 'balanced' or 'aligned' by the healing power of crystals. For Mark Chipperfield, who was admittedly somewhat sceptical, crystal healing had no tangible effect at all and any potential benefit was somewhat undermined by the accusing tone of the therapist he visited. 'It's a wonder you're still walking around' she told him. 'For a start, your third eye is turning completely inwards and your chakras are almost not working at all.'[15]

In fairness to the less gimmicky aspects of the New Age, however, it must be acknowledged that there are also other approaches and techniques which have much greater claim to recognition and acceptance. One can gauge their respective merits not in terms of the 'quick cosmic fix' provided by channelled advice and crystal healing, but through their capacity to assist enduring personal transformation. These approaches, which include meditation, rebirthing, shamanic visualisation, holotropic breathing and the float-tank experience, all offer potential access to states of archetypal and spiritual awareness and may be described cumulatively as 'pathways to transpersonal consciousness'. They clearly represent the 'cutting edge' of the New Age.

Approaches to Transpersonal States of Consciousness

Meditation

Of the approaches mentioned above, meditation is undoubtedly the most familiar and widespread. Nevertheless, it is also frequently misunderstood.

A popular misconception about meditation is that it is a type of passive introversion, a peaceful but ineffectual form of self-centredness. In fact meditation is quite different from this and as a technique of mind control has very positive benefits for health. Those who practise meditation systematically and regularly believe it leads to increased inner calm, heightened powers of creativity and decision making, increased efficiency in the work situation and decreased mental tension and negative emotions.

The meditative approach to life is not confined to any one spiritual belief system or religion and is found in different forms in Buddhism, Hinduism, Sufism and Christianity. Essentially meditation produces heightened powers of awareness and deep feelings of tranquillity, and represents a type of journey into the inner self.

Meditation has become increasingly popular in the West, partly as a result of the TM movement and the many forms of yoga now readily available. Millions of people in the United States have learned some form of meditation and the practice is also very popular in Britain, Europe, Australia and other Western countries.

The appeal of meditation is that it broadens one's sense of being. As Baba Ram Dass has said, 'Meditation frees your awareness' and opens new horizons of perception. There are basically two approaches to meditation. The first focuses on powers of concentration, the second emphasises detached awareness.

The 'concentration' approach requires that the attention be focused on a meditative symbol, a sound or chant, or a body process like breathing. Sometimes sacred mantras are also used, and in some forms of meditation such mantras are provided personally by the teacher to the pupil — the latter then meditates on that mantra at different times of the day. The idea is to turn the processes of thought inwardly until the mind transcends thought itself.

In the second approach, of 'detached awareness', the focus is on what is happening *now*. The task is not so much to elevate consciousness to a 'higher state' but to become increasingly aware of the present moment. From that position one gains an awareness of the flux of life and the ebb and flow of human experience.

The *Visuddhimagga* — the Path to Purification — by the 5th century monk Buddhaghosa, describes the meditative approach from the Buddhist viewpoint. One of the major disciplines of the Buddhist meditator is to eliminate distractions, with the aim of attaining 'unification of mind'. As the practitioner learns to meditate for a long period of time, such factors as agitation, scepticism and doubt disappear and a feeling of one-pointedness (bliss) begins to dominate. The meditator becomes absorbed in thought — a process known as *jhana* — and moves deeper and deeper, finally acquiring an awareness of infinite space. Many Buddhists, however, regard the pursuit of various *jhana* levels as secondary to the Path of Mindfulness which leads, finally, to *nirvana*. The meditator learns to break out of stereotypes of thought and perceives every moment of the familiar reality as if it were a new event. The ego becomes comparatively less important and the manifested universe is seen to be in a state of total and ever-changing flux. This leads to a sense of detachment from the world of experience, an abandonment of all desires and self-interest and finally the transcendence, or dissolution, of the ego itself.

Rebirthing

Rebirthing is a connected-breathing method which has become increasingly popular in the Holistic Health movement. Based on the Indian science of breath, *pranayama*, the rebirthing technique was developed by the Californian therapist Leonard Orr and has been further modified by Dr Stanislav Grof.

In a rebirthing session the subject relaxes and uses a breathing rhythm in which there is no pause between the in-breath and the out-breath. The facilitating therapist monitors this breathing pattern, which produces a hyperventilation effect and takes the subject into an altered state of consciousness.

The importance of breathing needs hardly be stressed but as the founder of Bioenergetics, Alexander Lowen, puts it: 'Breathing. . . provides the oxygen for the metabolic processes, literally it supports the fires of life. But breath as "pneuma" is also the spirit or soul. We live in an ocean of air like fish in a body of water. By our breathing we are attuned to our atmosphere. If we inhibit our breathing we isolate ourselves from the medium in which we exist. In all Oriental and mystic philosophies, the breath holds the secret to the highest bliss. This is why breathing is the dominant factor in the practice of yoga.'[16]

The basic idea behind rebirthing is to use the connected breathing technique to move towards a peak where the inner vibrational state either produces a blissful, liberating sensation or an emotional block-age which the subject needs to pass through. The 'rebirth' occurs when the subject overcomes any subconscious traumas which emerge at this time. Leonard Orr believes that at this stage the person can look within for what he calls the 'inner divinity': 'You merge with your breath, flowing, glowing, soaring, relaxing profoundly, your mind melting into your spirit, surging, awakening your inner being and the quiet sounds of your soul.'

For Grof the process is beneficial primarily because it produces a state of catharsis:

> 'Intense breathing, continued for a period of about thirty to forty-five minutes, tends to collect the tensions in the body into a stereotyped pattern of armouring, and eventually releases them. . . In this tech-nique, vocalisation and conventional abreaction is generally discour-aged and the subject is asked to continue breathing until all the tensions are released.'[17]

Rebirthing is therefore both therapeutic and aesthetic. It is usually performed in a private room with gentle music and a supportive at-mosphere, with the subject lying on a mat (this technique is known as 'dry rebirthing'). However rebirthing can also be applied in a hot-tub where the subject floats naked face-down in warm water, wears a snor-kel and nose-clip, and maintains the continuous breath-cycle. The sub-ject gradually 'surrenders his ego' to the surroundings and may have an experience relating the to the unity of the foetus within the womb. The subject is then lifted by the therapist out of the hot-tub onto a nearby mat, covered with blankets, and allowed to flow into the medi-tative state which follows (this variant is called 'wet rebirthing').

Holotropic Breathing
Holotropic Breathing is a development from Rebirthing, formulated by Dr Grof, and is intended to produce more intense and dramatic breakthroughs to transpersonal states of consciousness. Grof coined the term 'holotropic', meaning 'growing towards wholeness'.

Here the breathing cycle is accompanied by recorded music which is chosen to reflect different phases of the cathartic process. As Grof explains: 'The music is the vehicle itself, so at the beginning we start with some very activating, powerful music. Then, maybe an hour into the session, we move into a kind of culminating, "breakthrough" type of music — for example using the sounds of bells or similar, very powerful transcendental sounds.' His musical selections are very varied, including African tribal rhythms, Sufi chants, Indian ragas, Japanese flutes and various forms of ambient New Age music.

Grof makes the point that hyperventilation breathing reduces the amount of oxygen transmitted to the cortex of the brain, producing a natural 'high'. The Holotropic experience opens out into the transpersonal dimension and, can be 'very beneficial, very transforming and very healing. Many people tell us after a session like this that they have never been so relaxed in their whole life'.[18]

Shamanic Visualisation

Introduced to the Human Potential Movement in the 1970s by American anthropologist Dr Michael Harner, shamanic healing incorporates visualisation techniques within a 'ceremonial' setting. Harner's field-research in the early 1960s took him among both the South American and North American Indians, including the Jivaro of the Ecuadorian Andes, the Wintun, Pomo, Coast Salish, Conibo and Lakota Sioux, and it was among these peoples that he learned shamanism first-hand. The method he presents is essentially a synthesis adapted for a Western audience, while still remaining true to the principles of mainstream shamanism.

Harner's workshops — presented mainly at meetings organised by the International Transpersonal Association, at Esalen Institute and other personal growth centres in the United States and Europe feature the beating of a large flat drum which the person taking the role of the shamanic voyager uses as a vehicle to travel into the 'mythic world'. The participant relaxes in darkness, or with the eyes closed, and visualises a majestic tree whose branches reach up towards the heavens and whose roots extend deep into the earth. As the drumming begins, the technique is to imagine that you are entering a doorway at the foot of the tree and then feel as if you are passing into one of the large roots — which then becomes a tunnel through to light which is perceived at the other end. The shaman now journeys towards the light, feeling all the time that the drumbeat is providing a sense of propulsion, and passes through into the luminous haze beyond. At this stage the participant now 'calls' for a guide — an animal, spirit being or mythic creature — who can assist in the exploration of the shamanic realm of consciousness which is now accessible. The journey lasts for around twenty minutes, although one often has the feeling that the journey is 'beyond time', and ends when a special drumbeat signal calls the voyager home.

Harner believes that the monotonous drum rhythms produced during a shamanic session activates theta patterns in the brain (associated with creative thought) and also simulates the rhythmic beating of the heart. In an interview in 1984 he compared shamanic states of mind with the realms of consciousness accessed through Zen meditation:

'There have been very few scientific studies so far on what happens to a shaman making the journey. We need much more of this kind of research. But in one research project that was done using electroencephalographic equipment to measure brain-waves, it was found that the shaman in just ten minutes of journeying achieved a state of consciousness, empirically, scientifically measured, that had only been duplicated once before and that was by Japanese Zen masters in deep meditation after six hours of work. So the effect of the drumming, as well as the shamanic methods, is very, very considerable.'[19]

Shamanic visualisation can be used as a method of self-exploration, for one often uncovers archetypal or spiritual dimensions of one's being during such altered states of consciousness, but shamanism also has a healing role. An individual shaman, sometimes accompanied by a small 'support group', will make a spirit-journey on behalf of a patient who feels ill, or dis-spirited, and may be able to find an energy source to transmit into that person's body. For the recipient of shamanic healing the 'shamanising' can produce a dramatic emotional transformation at this time, and it may be that the subject performs a spontaneous dance or some other ritual act, by way of thanking, and making welcome, the healing energy which has now been bestowed.

Michael Harner believes that the mythic and 'symbolic' experiences which arise during shamanic visualisation sessions reveal a dimension of consciousness rarely accessed in daily life:

'Simply by using the technique of the drumming, people from time immemorial have been able to pass into realms which are normally reserved for those approaching death, or for saints. These are the realms of the upper and lower world where one can get information to puzzling questions. This is the Dreamtime of the Australian aboriginal, the "mythic time" of the shaman. In this area, a person can obtain knowledge that rarely comes to other people.'[20]

One woman in a Harner workshop had a mythic experience which is typical of the shamanic spirit-journey:

'I was flying. I went up into black sky — there were so many stars and then I went into an area that was like a whirlwind. I could still see the stars and I was turning a lot, and my power animals were with me.

Then I came up through a layer of clouds and met my teacher — who was a woman I'd seen before. She was dressed in a long, long gown and I wanted to ask her how I could continue with my shamanic work, how to make it more a part of my daily life. Then she took me up through her vagina, actually took me into her, into her belly. I could feel her get pregnant with me and felt her belly stretching. I felt myself inside her. I also felt her put her hands on top of her belly, and how large it was ! She told me that I should stop breathing, that I should take nourishment from her, and I could actually feel myself stop breathing. I felt a lot of warmth in my belly, as if it were coming into me, and then she stretched further and actually broke apart. Her belly broke apart and I came out of her, and I took it to mean that I needed to use less will in my work, and that I needed to trust her more and let that enter my daily life. That was the end of my journey — the drum stopped and I came back at that point.'[21]

Experiences of this sort beg the question of whether the shaman's journey is just imagination. Is the mythic experience *really* real? Harner's reply is persuasive:

'Imagination is a modern Western concept that is outside the realm of shamanism. "Imagination" already prejudges what is happening. I don't think it is imagination as we ordinarily understand it. I think we are entering something which, surprisingly, is universal regardless of culture . . . For the shaman, what one sees — that's real. What one reads out of a book is second-hand information. But just like the scientist, the shaman depends upon first-hand observation to decide what's real. If you can't trust what you see yourself, then what can you trust?'[22]

The Float-Tank Experience

The idea of floating naked in a sensory isolation tank in order to relax or explore transpersonal states of consciousness is not yet a mainstream practice, although there are now increasing numbers of float-tank centres in our cities and suburbs.

The original sensory isolation tanks were pioneered by neuro-physiologist Dr John Lilly over thirty years ago, when he was working for the National Institute of Mental Health in Bethesda, Maryland. Lilly's idea was to produce an environment of solitude, isolation and confinement where sensory input was minimised as far as was humanly possible, and to see what happened. Wearing a special latex rubber mask fitted with a breathing apparatus, Lilly floated naked in quiet solitude and darkness, in sea-water heated to a constant 93°F, the temperature at which one is neither hot nor cold. In the darkness Lilly felt as if he were floating in a gravity-free dimension. He discovered that the brain compensates for the reduction of sensory stimulation by producing a marked degree of heightened inner awareness. 'I went through dream-like states, trance-like states, mystical states,' he wrote later. 'In all of those states I was totally intact.' He remained simultaneously aware of his floating body and the nature of the experiment.

This inquiry into sensory isolation was Lilly's first scientific contact with mystical reality. It seemed to him that under these conditions the brain, or 'bio-computer', released a particular 'programme' of sensory experiences. The programme would be directly related to one's concepts and beliefs. That is to say, one would only perceive things within the grasp of the imagination. A person with narrow conceptual confines would find himself in a barren, constricting 'space' when his mind-contents were revealed to him.

During one of his mystical experiences, Lilly — who had been raised as a devout Roman Catholic — found himself experiencing the 'flight of the soul'. He saw angelic beings and an aged patriarchal God seated on a throne. A religious belief programme from his youth had been re-activated! 'Later' wrote Lilly, 'I was to realise that the limits of one's belief set the limit of the experience.'[23]

Lilly found through his sensory isolation experiments that such states offered, potentially, tremendous freedom. With external 'reality' excluded, one could programme a mental journey to any place which the imagination could conceive — the choice of programme would take you to different inner 'spaces', states of consciousness representing various states of transcendence.

Lilly subsequently introduced his friend, actor Burgess Meredith, to the tank experiments and he too experienced much the same thing. In a recent interview he said: 'Tanking is a purely restful experience. It's a type of meditation where you alter your state of thinking. It becomes apparent to you that there are other things in life besides action. Floating renews your thinking process. . .'[24]

When Lilly's account of his tank experiences, *The Centre of the Cyclone*, was published in 1972, it achieved something of a cult following and one of its admirers was a computer programmer named Glenn Perry. Perry proposed that Lilly modify his design and replace the sea-salt with Epsom salts that had no effect on the skin or hair. The new tank was around four feet high and also had an air pump to improve the circulation. Later Perry and Lilly formed the Samadhi Tank company and isolation tanks were made available to the public for the first time.

These days the float tanks are even more sophisticated. They are attractively coloured to remove any feelings of paranoia or claustrophobia, and some models are wired for ambient music, which is fed into the chamber as an additional meditative support. The isolation process is undoubtedly a powerful and effective way of encountering the mind. One has the option of employing one's solitude simply as a means of relaxation and contemplation, or drifting off into the peaceful void beyond. As Lilly himself has said it is simply a matter of exploring the boundaries of one's own imagination and personal belief systems. Where the inner journey takes us is essentially in our own hands.

Sacred Psychology and the Rise of the Feminine

One of the most important impulses that characterises the New Age is the rising interest in Sacred Psychology and the Feminine 'mythic principle' which is now permeating into popular consciousness.

Acknowledgement of the Feminine takes many different forms. It may be expressed through the sacred metaphor of Gaia — embodiment of the living planet and the increasing global environmental awareness — or it may be through the 'Jungian' perception that a male-dominated society should learn to acquire the 'feminine' gifts of nurturing and intuition. And it is mirrored, too, in the revival of interest in the esoteric Wiccan and Neopagan traditions which honour the Universal Goddess through different ritual expressions.

Such directions in our society are hardly surprising. As the international feminist movement helped rectify an imbalance in the sociopolitical sphere during the 1960s and '70s, it was surely only a matter of time before such expressions flowed through into different forms of feminine spirituality.

Margot Adler, granddaughter of the famous psychologist Alfred Adler, embodies this principle perfectly. A reporter for National Public Radio in New York, and the acclaimed author of *Drawing Down the Moon*, Adler says that she first fell in love with the Greek gods and goddesses when she was 12 years of age. Now an initiated Wiccan and, spokesperson for the Neopagan movement in the United States, she feels strongly that the esoteric mystical traditions provide the opportunity for direct spiritual experience.

In an interview published in *East West* in October 1984 she told journalist Victoria Williams that Wicca involved 'seeing the earth as sacred, seeing human beings and everything else as part of that creation, seeing divinity as immanent and not transcendent, and seeing people as basically good'. She told me much the same thing when I interviewed her in New York for a television documentary:

'I think that one of the reasons that so many people in the United States have come to paganism is that they see in it a way of resacralising the world, of making it animated, of making it vivid again, of having a relationship to it that allows for harmony and wholeness. Perhaps this can help create a world that is more harmonious with Nature and can end the despoliation of the planet.'[25]

However she also indicated that one of the areas where Wicca differed from more organised religions was in emphasising that the divine principle could be found, potentially, within every living person — a formal structure or belief system was not required.

'The fundamental thing about the magical and pagan religions' said Margot Adler, 'is that ultimately they say. . . Within yourself you are the god, you are the goddess — you can actualise within yourself and create whatever you need on this earth and beyond.'[26]

Also a key figure in the Wiccan movement is Miriam Simos, otherwise known as Starhawk, a San Francisco-based writer, counsellor and political activist. Author of *The Spiral Dance* and *Dreaming the Dark*, Starhawk studied feminism at UCLA. She regards her magical craft as the ability to transform consciousness at will and believes the female practitioner has a special and privileged role. As a representative of the Goddess, the female Wiccan is, metaphorically, a giver of life:

The images of the Goddess as birth-giver, weaver, earth and growing plant, wind and ocean, flame, web, moon, and milk, all speak to me of connectedness, sustenance, healing, creating.

If you think of magic as an art, art implies imagery and vision. The basic principle of magic is that you work with visualisation, making pictures in your mind through which you direct energy. Ritual is simply a patterned movement of energy that opens the channels to the marvellous living force we are all part of. Magical systems are highly elaborate metaphors, and through them we can identify ourselves and connect with larger forces. If magic is the art of causing change in accordance with will, then political acts, acts that speak truth to power, that push for change, are acts of magic. My model of power says that the world itself is sacred and the Goddess is simply our name for the living organism of which we're all a part.'[27]

This type of mythic perception, however, extends well beyond the occult traditions of Wicca and 'Women's Mysteries'. Two other advocates of mythic renewal — Dr Jean Shinoda Bolen and Dr Jean Houston — have both come to a similar position from quite different initial perspectives.

Dr Bolen is a Jungian psychiatrist and author of such works as Goddesses in *Everywoman, Gods in Everyman* and *The Tao of Psychology*. For many years she has been advocating that each of us can apply the archetypal energies of the Gods and Goddesses in our lives.

Bolen trained as a doctor, was strongly influenced by the women's movement in the 1960s and taught a course on the psychology of women at the University of California's San Francisco campus. She is now Clinical Professor of Psychiatry at the University of California Medical Center. Bolen believes, like Jung, that myths are a path to the deeper levels of the mind:

> 'Myth is a form of metaphor. It's the metaphor that's truly empowering for people. It allows us to see our ordinary lives from a different perspective, to get an intuitive sense of who we are and what is important to us. . . Myths are the bridge to the collective unconscious. They tap images, symbols, feelings, possibilities and patterns — inherent, inherited human potential that we all hold in common.'[28]

While, for some, myths may perhaps have an archaic, distant quality that hardly seems relevant. In everyday reality, Bolen argues quite the opposite. For her, a mythic or archetypal awareness can provide a real sense of meaning in day-to-day life:

> 'If you live from your own depths — that is, if there is an archetypal basis for what you're doing — then there's a meaningful level to it that otherwise might be missing. . . When people "follow their bliss" as Joseph Campbell says, their heart is absorbed in what they're doing. People who work in an involved, deep way are doing something that matters to them just to be doing it, not for the paycheck, not for someone saying to them: "What a good job you're doing.'[29]

In her own life, and despite her Japanese ancestry, Jean Shinoda Bolen has identified, like Margot Adler, with the Greek goddesses. She told interviewer Mirka Knaster that, for her, the goddesses who had most reflected in her life were Artemis, Athena and Hestia — who represented the 'independent, self-sufficient qualities in women'. Artemis, Goddess of the Hunt, seemed to embody her Japanese family's frequent moves around the United States in the 1940s to avoid being detained in an American concentration camp. Athena, Goddess of Wisdom, seemed present in her decision to train as a medical doctor, and Hestia, Goddess of the Hearth, epitomised her present love of 'comfort in solitude'.

However, as a writer and lecturer, she has also felt drawn to Hermes, as an archetype of communication, and was at pains to point out that we can all embody both the gods *and* goddesses in our lives — not just the archetypes of our own gender. And, most significantly, she sees such mythic attunement as opening out into greater, planetary awareness. Echoing the sentiments of both Margot Adler and Starhawk, she explains that:

> 'The current need is a return to earth as the source of sacred energy. I have a concept that I share with others that we're evolving into looking out for the earth and our connection with everybody on it. Women seem more attuned to it, but increasingly more men are too. I believe that the human psyche changes collectively, when enough individuals change. Basically, the point of life is to survive and evolve. To do both requires that we recognise our planetary community and be aware that we cannot do anything negative to our enemies without harming ourselves. I think that we may be evolving but then, I'm an optimistic soul.'[30]

Dr Jean Houston, also a strong advocate of archetypal psychology, takes much the same position, and is similarly attuned to the new 'Gaia consciousness'. 'The Earth is a living system' she says. 'That is why women are now being released from the exclusivity of a child-bearing, child-rearing role. This is also the time when the Earth desperately needs the ways of thinking and being that women have developed through hundreds of thousands of years.' Jean Houston is a former president of the Association for Humanistic Psychology and director of the Foundation for Mind Research in Pomona, New York, but her talents also extend into creative spiritual expression. An award-winning actress in Off-Broadway theatre, she has developed training programmes in spiritual studies which include the enactment of themes from the ancient Mystery traditions. She also trained as a classics scholar in ancient languages and has a background in psychedelic research. She co-authored *The Varieties of Psychedelic Experience* and *Psychedelic Art* in the late 1960s and her more recent books include *The Possible*

Human and *The Search for the Beloved.*

Houston is especially intrigued by the role that myth can play in shaping consciousness, and for several years has been working with the themes in Sacred Psychology. Of particular interest to her are the sacred journeys of human transformation — including such figures as Parsifal and the Holy Grail, St Francis, Odysseus, Christ and Isis — for all of these are examples of how we may undertake a quest of spiritual renewal.

In an article published in *Dromenon* in 1981 she explained that:

'In my work I try to teach people how to repattern and extend the uses of brain, body and symbolic knowing in order that they may become adequate vehicles for their own powerful psyches.'[31]

One of her techniques at this time was to ask participants to learn 'shape shiftings' by relaxing and identifying with different 'god-identities' thereby acquiring archetypal perceptions. Such roles might include meditating on such figures as the Great Mother, the Wise Old King, the Young Redeemer, the Trickster or the Holy Child.

But Houston now emphasises that such visualisations in themselves are not enough. It may well be that some sense of personal conflict is required to spur one on in the spiritual quest. Personal growth, she feels, can grow from the sense of being 'wounded' expressed, perhaps, in the feeling of being abandoned or hurt in some way. 'God' she says, 'may reach us through our affliction. . . we can be ennobled and extended by looking at this wounding in such a way that we move from the personal particular to the personal universal.'[32]

She expanded on these ideas in a recent interview in *Magical Blend:*

'So much of my work is. . . essentially a form of Sacred Theatre. I take the great stories, like Psyche and Eros, or Oedipus, or Faust, any of the stories of the Hero with a Thousand Faces or the Heroine, Demeter and Persephone, the Gnostic Sophia. . . There's something about the Great Story or the Great Myth that moves you beyond your personal particularity into the personal universal. Suddenly, you have not just brought a context and larger capacities; you literally take on the eyes of Athena, the taste buds of Dionysius, the yearning of Odysseus for home, the passion of Parsifal for the Grail. These large emotions are evoked in you because you are really part of a Larger Story, just as we are part of the air we breathe and the environment that we are in.'[33]

Houston also likes very much to work in groups for she has found, experientially, that this helps to awaken in each person the sense of participating in a mythic reality:

> 'We need the symbiosis with others. That's why I like to work in groups
> . . . There's more to share, more images. There are more aspects and
> alternatives, so more can happen. Group energy helps us grow.'[34]

The Journey of Human Potential

The essential message which emerges from thinkers like Margot Adler, Starhawk, Jean Shinoda Bolen and Jean Houston is that we should all endeavour to learn ways of tapping the sacred potential which is latent within our being. Various forms of ritual, theatre, ceremonial, meditation and visualisation can all assist this process but, at heart, the task for each of us is to rediscover the spiritual and universal in the everyday experience. This then becomes very much a personal quest — our own individual journey of the spirit. During our lifetime this may lead us along many different paths and through the company of many other guides and teachers, until we glimpse a perspective that is real for us: a situation in which the universal, as Jean Houston says, becomes particular to our own experience.

There is a clear message here for each of us, for if the process is to be a journey of true self-discovery, we should all endeavour to awaken our spiritual potential in the most instinctual ways we can find, allowing the sacred to rise up from within our inner depths rather than submerging ourselves in imposed belief systems. There is an implicit message here, too, for devotees of institutionalised or doctrinaire forms of religious belief and also new religious groupings headed by dominant 'gurus' and other spiritual leaders. The questions we should all ask are: Does my present 'spiritual path' allow me to grow in my perspectives? Does it open me to ever larger, more transcendent realms of spiritual experience? Or am I being limited by my present belief system and thereby, consciously or unconsciously, imposing barriers which define an enclosed and secure 'spiritual reality' I feel safe with? In the final analysis there is no-one who can supply these answers but ourselves.

8
Contemporary Shamanism and the Earth Mother

As the world's earliest religious expression — predating Vedism and Yoga, and extending back to the Palaeolithic era — shamanism is a widespread tradition which is still found as far afield as the United States and Mexico, Central and South America, Japan, Tibet, Indonesia, Aboriginal Australia and Nepal.

Shamanism is a visionary practice which focuses on the energies of Nature and provides a holistic balance between humankind and the Universe — shamans utilise altered states of consciousness to contact the gods and spirits of the natural world. When we think of the shaman, the image of an enigmatic and mysterious medicine man or sorceress comes to mind — a figure who, through entering a condition of trance, is able to undertake a vision-quest of the soul, journey to the sacred places and report back on matters of cosmic intent. It may be that the shaman is a healer, able to conquer the spirits of disease, a sorcerer, skilled in harnessing spirits as allies for magical purposes, or a type of psychic detective able to recover lost possessions. At other times, the shaman may seem to be somewhat priestlike — an intermediary between the gods of Creation and the more familiar realm of everyday domestic affairs. But whatever the specific role, the shaman, universally, is one who commands awe and respect, for the shaman can journey to other worlds and return with revelations from the gods.

The shamans here are all from the United States, although each is working in a different area and has different cultural affiliations. In North America, shamanism is found, for example, in Alaskan Eskimo society, among the Tlingit of the northwest coast, among the Paviotso hunters, fishers and gatherers from western Nevada, among the Mescalero and Chiricahua Apache hunters of Texas, Arizona and New Mexico, the Lakota Sioux of Dakota and also the Nez Perce, Chippewa,

143

Zuni and Twana. Shamanic traditions still survive, too, among the Pacific Coast Indians like the Pomo and Salish, the Chumash who formerly occupied the region around Ojai, and native tribes like the Yurok, Wintun and Karok of northwestern California.

So shamanism is reasonably widespread — even in a country as technologically developed as the United States. Indeed, we can see the resurgence of interest in shamanism as symptomatic of the widespread current perception that we should seek to return to the basics of life, return to our 'mythic origins' in Nature.

Shamanism urges us to recognise the sanctity of Nature and to find the god, and goddess, within ourselves — to seek for a healing balance of male and female energies within our being. Shamanism is a religious perspective which venerates Nature and — in this modern era of Chernobyl, industrial pollution and the ever-threatening chlorofluorocarbon hole within the ozone layer — shamanism encourages us to attune our beliefs to working with Nature, not against her. Although we, in the West, should not pretend to be Red Indians, even in our own, largely urban, context we can each act as a type of modern shaman by adopting this approach in our personal life. It is not so much a matter of theatre or ceremonial, but a shift in basic attitudes. Shamanism can teach us much, simply by leading us back to a core simplicity in our lives: the basic perception that we all share a common destiny on this planet, that we are all born of Mother Earth and that, ultimately, we are accountable, both to each other and to future generations, if the precious balance between humanity and Nature is jeopardised.

So it is worth heeding what the shamans have to say. The following perspectives from Luisah Teish, Brooke Medicine Eagle and Sun Bear — all well-known contemporary shamans encompass a philosophy of life that we can truly take to heart:

Luisah Teish
Now in her early forties, Luisah Teish was born in New Orleans of mixed African, Haitian, Choctaw and French ancestry and brings to her spiritual perspective a diverse range of influences. Raised in New Orleans, nominally a Roman Catholic but increasingly as a practitioner of Voudou, she is now also a priestess of the Nigerian Yoruba religion *Lucumi*. But this is not all. Today she is a dancer, a choreographer, a singer, a shaman, a healer, and a writer — her book *Jambalaya: The Natural Woman's Book of Personal Charms and Practical Rituals*

was published in San Francisco in 1985.

Teish (pronounced 'Teesh') — as she likes to be called — describes herself as originally `Louisiana Catholic': a polite expression for one who follows Voudou with a thin veneer of Christianity over the top.

It wasn't a case of deliberately pursuing magic, Teish told me when I first met her in California in 1984, so much as waiting for it to happen. The elders would perform secret rites around her as she was growing up and watch for omens, or for significant traits to emerge in her personality. Teish's mother wanted her to be a nurse or a teacher, and would ignore her questions about 'women's mysteries'. Nevertheless, Teish found she had an innate capacity for prophetic dreams and would frequently sleepwalk. She learnt magical cures by fossicking around for bits of information, and also gleaned insights into occult ways of reading weather patterns and interpreting animal behaviour. Teish explained that there is a paranoid element among Voudou practitioners in the deep south because practising traditional African religion on the slave plantations was punishable by death. Voudou instead became incorporated into domestic routine that wouldn't be noticed by the slave owners.

Teish recounts a fascinating event from her youth:

'When I was a little girl my mother used to send me to the Catholic church and she would tell me, "Go and ask Father Fitzpatrick for a little holy water." You know, she'd send me with a jar and I'd go get the holy water from the church, and she'd put it in a bucket with sugar, urine and a little perfume. Then she'd get a picture of one of the saints and mop the floor, and the whole time she was mopping the floor she was telling the saint what she wanted to have happening in her house — magically that is. That's what I call being 'Louisiana Catholic', where you're Catholic on the surface but there's a lot more going on underneath.'[1]

Teish says that her 'entire childhood was filled with visions and intuitions and the whispered guidance of a spirit guide whom I call "She Who Whispers"'. Psychic forces raged inside her and did not begin to manifest fully until her early twenties when she decided to confront her mother about her magical practices by tricking her into becoming a confidante. Teish announced that she was going to make a magical charm with graveyard dust. Her mother clearly recognised that Teish was ready for the secrets, and confided to her daughter that she was a medium and a member of an 'altar circle'. They have been 'good buddies' ever since.

Teish also says that learning dance with Katherine Dunham's group in the late 1960s helped her to free her psychic energies. Dunham had worked as an anthropologist, preserving the native dance traditions of Africa and Haiti, and Teish found that by working with her and performing these dances she was able to tap the primal impulses of her ancestral heritage. During one particular dance — *Damballoh* — she had an out-of-the body experience.

Some time after this, Teish joined the Fahami Temple of the Egyptian sun-god Amun-Ra and underwent a lengthy initiation which helped her appreciate her African spiritual roots even more. Her specific orientation is now the Lucumi tradition of West Africa.

For Luisah Teish the spiritual universe offers contact with the consciousness of the ancestors — called Eguns — and the consciousness of Nature — called Orishas. Eguns have lived before on the planet but Orishas are elemental energies in Nature like the river, wind, fire and ocean. Each Orisha has its own power, but some take a role of special prominence. Yemaya, for example, is the Mother of the Earth Spirits, a personification of the ocean, dreams, healing and cleansing. Teish says her mystery is unfathomable — 'Nobody knows what's at the bottom of the ocean' — but at the same time she feels a very close and respectful relationship with her: 'She is incredibly beautiful, incredibly powerful and wise.' Then there is the sky-god Obatala, representing the clouds, creativity, and the wisdom that comes with old age. He, too, is a friend. In fact, Teish says of the Orishas that 'the entire pantheon is so human that you don't feel like you are bowing to a superior. You feel like you have a relative or a friend with extra human powers who can help you.'

However, Teish's special bond is with Oshun, the Nigerian counterpart of the Roman goddess Venus, who is known also as 'Mother of the Spirit'. As Teish told writer Mimi Albert:

'I am a child of Oshun . . . I will sing the praise of Oshun all day long. Oshun is a river goddess, the goddess of the sweet waters. She is also the goddess of love . . . Oshun's colour is the bright yellow of illumination and wealth; her favourite foods are very sweet, very seedy, very leafy. Pumpkin, with all the seeds inside and its bright orange colour, is one of her foods; she also loves pastries and sweets and fruits of all kinds. She's the goddess of cooking, among other things, so we associate a well-laid table, with flowers, candles and gourmet dishes, with Oshun.'[2]

According to Teish, the Goddess lies asleep in the crown chakra — the psychic energy centre in the head. When a person is ritually initiated,

the magical herbs and songs arouse the spirit, and the devotee is pos-
sessed by Goddess. For her, magical dance in a Goddess ceremony has
a very powerful effect. As she explains, it induces a state of trance and
also the feeling of being out of the body:

> Suddenly I find I'm dancing off-rhythm, and an ancestor or a spirit is
> there. You are bombarded by music, and not really in control of your
> body. It seems that the drummer's hands are your feet and then at some
> point there is a great silence. You find you are now on the wall, on the
> ceiling — over there somewhere — watching your body performing . .
> . It's very invigorating. The body seems to be able to do things, in
> trance, that you cannot do when you're fully conscious. Bursts of en-
> ergy come in and take over!'[3]

Teish's magic is mostly benevolent and people come to her for spiritual advice, or for wealth and love charms. She claims to be able to
reverse black magic, but rarely inflicts harmful magic on others. 'Before doing that,' she says with a grin, 'I'd have to check with the god!'

However, Teish believes her main role is now to help others tune
into a universal religious awareness that goes beyond sectarian differences and recognises spirituality as a global phenomenon. She maintains that the true meaning of the word *Voudou* is 'life-force' and says
that her shamanic perspective focuses on helping to build an environmental understanding that acknowledges the sanctity of Nature. 'I do
have a basic faith in Nature's tendency to survive' she said recently,
reflecting on the near tragedy of Chernobyl. '. . . The closer we get to
the possibility of total destruction, the more Nature will cause a change
in basic consciousness to come about.'[4]

Brooke Medicine Eagle

Brooke Medicine Eagle provides an interesting example of how shamanism can link the old and the new — her lineage and ancestry point
back towards the traditional ways of the American Indians but she
has also been educated at a western university and has utilised various
holistic health therapies in formulating her world-view. She sees herself as, and indeed she is, a bridge between different cultures.

Brooke Medicine Eagle is of Sioux and Nez Perce extraction, although she was raised on the Crow Reservation in Montana. The
great-great-grandniece of Nez Perce holy man, Grandfather Joseph,
Brooke Medicine Eagle was brought up in very modest circumstances
and in comparative isolation. Together with her parents and brother,
she lived ten miles from the closest reservation village and nearly sixty

miles over dirt road from any major town. She says that the initial desire to be a healer-shaman came substantially from within her own experience.

On the other hand, Brooke Medicine Eagle's links with western culture came mostly through her education. She won a scholarship to the University of Denver, graduated with a Bachelor degree in psychology and mathematics and then earned a Master's in psychology, specialising in counselling. Since then she has also been strongly influenced by the bodywork approach of Moshe Feldenkrais and by the system of neurolinguistic programming formulated by Dr John Grinder and Richard Bandler. The way these helped her shamanic perspective is quite fascinating.

Moshe Feldenkrais was a Russian-born Israeli educator who emphasised the importance of awareness in human functioning. Awareness, he believed, could not be taught verbally but had to be experienced. With this in mind, he developed a system of movements aimed at undoing the emotional and cultural programming inflicted on people from childhood and replacing it with new ways of expressing natural impulses. Those working with the Feldenkrais method often speak of feeling exhilarated and more alive in their movements.

For Brooke Medicine Eagle, this concept is also part of shamanism. She emphasises the importance of expanding beyond artificial boundaries and limitations of movement and has compared the experience of literally being 'fenced in' by western methods of defining land areas with the sheer joy of riding for twenty or thirty miles on horseback in her native Montana. For her, the western way of thinking tends often to be restrictive and inhibiting. 'Most of us think of life as a path,' she says, 'the best being the straight and narrow, where we can plod along without change. I think life is more like flying a glider.'[5]

Following on from this, one of the features of the group-work she now undertakes is an exercise in overcoming fear and literally 'flying' into the unknown. Brooke Medicine Eagle has, on her ranch, what she calls her 'high-challenge ropes course' which consists of a system of ropes, wires and balancing logs, many of them high above the ground. One particular platform is 55 feet high and it is connected to a zip-line which extends downward for some 500 feet. While there are in-built safety precautions, participants who mount the platform and leap off along the zip-line have to overcome their intense fears and also learn a new sense of poise and balance prior to leaping forth. It is a challenging but also exhilarating experience, and according to Brooke

Medicine Eagle its lessons are intrinsic to shamanic philosophy: 'The challenge is to play on the edge — the edge of the unformed. Part of the shaman's way is that exquisite balance — between light and dark, in an out, left and right, formless and formed.'[6]

Allied to her interest in Feldenkrais's system of Awareness Through Movement is her study of neuro-linguistic programming, or NLP. The term derives from the Greek word *neuron*, 'nerve' and the Latin, *lingua*, 'language' and indicates that there is a sensory factor in all forms of behaviour which in turn affects the structure and sequence of different forms of communication. The programming factor relates to habitual thought and behaviour patterns which affect certain outcomes.

Many forms of behaviour do not produce satisfactory outcomes and may lead to psychosomatic disease, aberrant perceptions of life, or states of being well below optimal levels of functioning. The NLP therapist observes the client's behavioural and linguistic patterns, and endeavours to guide the person beyond personal limitations to new levels of awareness and personal effectiveness.

For Brooke Medicine Eagle, NLP has highlighted the way that western culture leads, so often, to programming behaviour and perpetuating habits — as she says, 'putting a form on things'. The trouble with this is that the more we reside in our habitual behaviour patterns, the less able we are to be open to acquiring new knowledge. This, too, is where shamanism can be beneficial. 'My work' she says, 'is about finding ways to help us move as shamans have: to challenge the darkness; to awaken ourselves by breaking through daily habitual form into Spirit.' Speaking again in the metaphorical language she is fond of, she says we should all learn new ways of 'changing with the breeze, moving like water. If we hold tight to a form — any form — I think we lose it.'[7]

These aspects of her world-view notwithstanding, Brooke Medicine Eagle has also come through a traditional Native American initiatory process. Her actual name, which can also be written as Little-Sister-of-the-Eagle, came to her through dreams and visions, and more recently she has also been given a new spiritual name, Chalise, by her inner guides. This name means 'a chalice overflowing with light' 'My challenge' she says, 'is to truly become a chalice to receive and channel light.' She feels that one of her special spiritual tasks is to create 'a pillar of light that holds up the sky', and indeed, light is central to her vision of shamanism. 'As we lighten up in all ways, we become less

dense, more filled with Spirit. Earth and physical bodies are the dens-
est experience our eternal spirit can have; our challenge is to fill and
balance it with the lightness of Spirit.'[8]

Brooke Medicine Eagle took her shamanic vision quest with an 85-
year-old-Northern Cheyenne shamaness called The Woman Who
Knows. Together with a younger medicine-woman they journeyed to
a place called Bear Butte, near the Black Hills of South Dakota. This
region had been used for hundreds of years by the Sioux and Cheyenne
as a location for the vision-quest. Here Brooke Medicine Eagle underwent the traditional preparation of fasting and cleansing. She was ex-
pecting to spend up to four days and nights alone on a mountain top,
without food and water, praying for her initiatory vision.

After preparing a sage-bed, smoking a pipe and offering prayers,
the women departed and Brooke Medicine Eagle was left alone. She
recalls that in the evening, as she lay there peacefully, she suddenly
became aware of the presence of another woman who had long black
braided hair and was dressed in buckskin. She seemed to be imparting
some sort of energy into her navel — the communication between
them was not in words.

As clouds moved across the sky, allowing the moonlight to filter
through, Brooke Medicine Eagle became aware of 'a flurry of rain-
bows' caused by hundreds of beads on the woman's dress. Now she
could also hear drumming, and it seemed then that two circles of dancing women — 'spirits of the land' — surrounded her, and that these
circles were interweaving with each other. One circle included seven
old grandmothers, 'women who are significant to me, powerful old
women.'[9]

Then the circles disappeared and once again she was alone with the
Rainbow Woman. The woman now told her that the land was in
trouble — that it needed a new sense of balance, and specifically more
feminine, nurturing energy and less male aggression. She also said that
all dwellers on the North American continent were 'children of the
rainbow' — mixed-bloods — but that there could be a balancing between the old cultures and the new.

After they had spoken with each other in this way it was time for
the Rainbow Woman to leave, and it now became abundantly clear
that this being was a spirit teacher, not a tangible physical form:

'Her feet stayed where they were, but she shot out across the sky in a
rainbow arc that covered the heavens, her head at the top of that arc.
And then the lights that formed that rainbow began to die out, almost

like fireworks in the sky, died out from her feet and died out and died out. And she was gone.'[10]

For Brooke Medicine Eagle the impact of the visitation was both personal and profound, for the communication touched on the crucial distinction between Native American and Western ways, and also indicated how she could be of service.

'The Indian people are the people of the heart. When the white man came to this land, what he was to bring was the intellect, that analytic, intellectual way of being. And the Indian people were to develop the heart, the feelings. And those two were to come together to build a new age, in balance, not one or the other . . .

[The Rainbow Woman] felt that I would be it carrier of the message between the two cultures, across the rainbow bridge, from the old culture to the new, from the Indian culture to the dominant culture, and back again. And in a sense, all of this generation can be that. We can help bridge that gap, build that bridge into the new age of balance.'[11]

This, then, is Brooke Medicine Eagle's particular path in shamanism. It is a path she treads with a special conviction, sure in the knowledge that the earth will benefit from more feminine energy, more caring. 'We need to allow, to be receptive, to surrender, to serve,' she says. 'The whole society, men and women, need that balance to bring ourselves into balance.'

Sun Bear

A medicine-man of Chippewa descent, Sun Bear is by no means a typical shaman. He is comparatively New Age in his orientation, heads a communal organisation consisting mainly of non-Native Americans, has worked in Hollywood, has a thriving practice in workshops and vision-quests, and has written several books. And yet he is a man whose message has touched many hearts. As a medicine-man he feels, like Brooke Medicine Eagle, that his path is to reach out to other cultures and to share with them his vision for harmony on earth.

Sun Bear, or Gheezis Mokwa, was born in 1929 on the White Earth Reservation in northern Minnesota. As a young child he had a vision of a large black bear sheathed in a vivid array of rainbow colours. The bear looked steadfastly at him, stood on its hind legs and gently touched him on his head. In this way he got his name. He also learned native medicine ways from his uncles and his brothers but then left his reservation at the age of 15. He says he didn't actually practise the medicine path until he was 25 years old. Prior to that he had quite a different career. Sun Bear worked in the Midwest and Southwest pursuing an assortment of occupations, including farming fields and working variously in a cemetery, bakery and real estate office. However, all this time he was still studying Native American healing traditions.

Later he worked for ten years in Hollywood on such television programmes as *Brave Eagle, Broken Arrow* and *Bonanza* and had acting parts in several films. In 1961 he also began publishing a magazine called *Many Smokes* which was intended as a forum for Native American writers and as a means of assisting the ecological cause of Earth awareness. The magazine changed its name to *Wildfire* in 1983 and now publishes a broad range of articles, encompassing holistic health, vision-quests, wilderness studies, herbalism and New Age philosophy.

After working for the Intertribal Council of Nevada, as an economic development specialist, Sun Bear assisted in a Native Studies programme, sponsored by the University of California at Davis, north of San Francisco. It was here, in 1970, that he founded the Bear Tribe. Most of the members were his former students from the Davis campus. Sun Bear maintains that he selected the name because 'The Bear is one of the few animals that heals its own wounds' and he had in mind an organisation whose members 'could all join together to help with the healing of the Earth'.[12]

For a time, the Bear Tribe resided near Placerville, California, but it is now located on a 100-acre farm, amidst luxuriant evergreens, close to Vision Mountain, 35 miles from Spokane in Washington. Sun Bear often isn't there — he now has an international workshop schedule which has taken him as far afield as Germany, Holland, England, India and Australia — but he has several able assistants who help to maintain the momentum. These include his wife, Wabun, formerly Marlise Ann James — a Masters graduate from the Columbia School of Journalism — and Shawnodese, who worked as a health inspector in Idaho prior to organising the Bear Tribe's Medicine Wheel gatherings. The community in Spokane is largely self-sufficient, has an extensive range of livestock, grows much of its own food and encourages self-reliance. Its workshop programme is extensive — an estimated 10,000 people attend Bear Tribe programmes each year — and the organisation has a 30,000 mailing list. There is no doubting that The Bear Tribe is an impressive operation.

Likewise, it would be easy to dismiss Sun Bear as an opportunist who has blended American Indian culture and modern American capitalism. However, several factors tell against this. Firstly, he doesn't draw a salary and also, like other members of the Tribe, he assists in the menial tasks that have to be done on the farm. The Bear Tribe also offers work opportunities to the unemployed. Nevertheless, Sun Bear does not believe in turning his back on modern advances. 'I don't cling to any particular old way or ritual' he told journalist Robert Neubert, 'nor do I believe that technology is necessarily bad: it's the greed and misdirection of its users that does harm. So the Bear Tribe isn't going back to the Stone Age. It's moving forward into the New Age.'[13]

But what of Sun Bear's personal vision? To what extent does he align himself with the traditional medicine path?

Sun Bear has summed up his philosophy as being one which teaches others to 'walk in balance on the Earth Mother.' In his book *The Medicine Wheel* he says: 'We all share the same Earth Mother, regardless of race or country of origin, so let us learn the ways of love, peace and harmony and seek the good paths in life.'[14]

For Sun Bear it is no longer appropriate to restrict the Native American teachings only to his own people. His view is truly global and he feels very strongly that his message is one of helping restore a sense of balance, of increased ecological awareness:

'If you teach people to find a better balance within themselves, how to be stronger, centre their life, and go forward with a good balance upon the Earth Mother, then that is a healing. You take away all the little pains when you teach people to become self-reliant . . . When people have centred themselves, they know that they can draw power from the universe.'[15]

Despite his apparently New Age emphasis, Sun Bear draws strongly on authentic Native American traditions. He shows group participants how to undertake a vision-quest — which includes fasting, prayers and ritual cleansing in a sweat-lodge: 'a symbolic act of entering the womb of the Mother to be reborn.' Four days and nights are then spent on the sacred mountain in isolation — some try to stay awake during this time but others allow themselves to fall asleep, hoping that mystical revelations will appear in their dreams.

But underlying all this, as Sun Bear explains, is an attitude of openness. One has to be able to receive the spirit, to cast aside the old restrictive programming. Accordingly, one of the practices prior to journeying to the sacred mountain is to dig a hole, pour into it one's anger and frustration, and then cover the hole over again with dirt and a prayer. Then it is a matter of going to a location where Earth Mother feels strong, where the energy seems vibrant, and where spirits might appear. It is the presence of spirits, in dreams or in visions. that provides an authentic sense of personal direction. But largely this is up to oneself. As Sun Bear says: 'Each medicine-man has to follow his own medicine and the dreams and visions that give him power.'

Another way of attracting the spirits is to don an animal mask, for example that of a buffalo, bear or eagle. By doing this, one feels a strong surge of spiritual energy, a profound sense of transformation:

'You literally become that entity, that power... The spirit comes into you completely, to the extent that you are no longer there, and you are able to communicate what that spirit is feeling. That is what the ceremonies are about at the deepest depth.'[16]

One can definitely tell when the spirits have arrived, says Sun Bear: 'Sometimes it is just little whisperings, and sometimes a different energy, a change in the air that you feel: it is very recognisable.' One then begins to communicate on a different level of awareness: 'You feel and experience things as an energy that comes through the spirit forces at the time.'[17]

Sun Bear believes that, as a medicine-man, he is a protector of the Earth Mother, and an embodiment of the spirits of the earth. The resurgence of interest in shamanism is a reflection of the fact that humankind has increasingly fallen out of harmony with Nature. This is where Sun Bear feels he has a special role to play. His aim, when working with participants on a vision-quest, is 'to teach them how to make prayers and ceremonies for communication with the natural forces, so that they can start learning to restore their own power.'[18] Clearly, this is an endeavour from which we can all learn.

9
Sacred Plants and Mystic Realities :
An Interview with Terence McKenna

Terence McKenna is one of the most controversial and illuminating figures in the Human Potential Movement. Renowned for his special gift of eloquent dialogue he amazes his audiences with his eclectic references to shamanism, visionary literature, psychedelics and the mystical traditions. For his position on these matters is nothing short of revolutionary.

McKenna believes that the shamanic model of the Universe — undoubtedly the world's most archaic — is nevertheless the most accurate and that we should heed shamanic traditions and practices in our efforts to map the psyche.[1] He also believes that since research into the psychedelics has been banned by the authorities, valuable insights into the potentials of consciousness are in danger of being overlooked.

Could you describe the different phases of your spiritual quest — from the beginning?
My original impetus was the shamanism of Central Asia which, as an art historian in the late 1960s, interested me enormously. I went to Nepal to learn the Tibetan language and get an insight not into Buddhism — which came to Tibet in the 7th century — but into the indigenous shamanism, Bon-Po, which has been there since earliest times. I quickly satisfied myself, comparing the experiences and the art that I was seeing in Nepal with the sort of experiences that I had had as an undergraduate on the LSD culture of the mid-1960s, that there was no clear one-to-one mapping between the psychedelic experience and traditional systems of esoteric thought — even though Timothy Leary and Ralph Metzner had given great impetus to that idea by publishing a psychedelic guide based on *The Tibetan Book of the Dead.*
    I practised yoga when I lived in India and in the Seychelles and I came to feel that either I was too lumpen to ever reach enlightenment

by this means or this was essentially the repetition of historical formulae where the real object had long since been lost or forgotten. So I then looked at shamanic traditions in situations where there had been less acculturation with the ongoing sweep of civilisation — that meant either the remote islands of Indonesia or the Amazon. And I visited both places — the Indonesian outer islands first, beginning with Sumatra. Over ten months, I walked myself south and east visiting Sumba, Sumbawa, Timor, Flores, the Moluccas, Ceram, and Temate. I was supporting myself as a professional butterfly collector, having a wonderful time and confronting a puzzle that many, many botanists have commented upon, and that was the unexplained paucity of psychoactive plants in the Old World tropics.

For reasons which are not at all well understood, the South American tropics have a virtual monopoly on plants that produce hallucinogenic indoles. Trying to construct an evolutionary scenario that would concentrate these compounds in one continent over all others is a thankless task, but having determined that there was no plant-based indigenous shamanism in Indonesia, I then in 1970 went to South America for the first time. I had made a thorough ethnographic study of the Amazon Basin before I went. Thanks to the work of Richard Evans Schultes at Harvard University there is a compendious body of this sort of material. The principal hallucinogens of the Amazon Basin are tryptamines of one sort or another, usually activated by being taken in combination with harmine, a monoamine oxidase (MAO) inhibitor which stimulates aural impressions. This was very interesting because it seemed to imply a pharmacological sophistication among these indigenous peoples that was only surpassed in the west in the mid-1950s, when this MAO system was understood.

Anyway, we got down to South America and began experimenting with these things — *ayahuasca*, the 'visionary vine' that Richard Spruce had first encountered when he was there in 1853, and the tryptamine-containing snuffs of the Waika and Yanomamo people. It was very clear to me that the experience of LSD in a profane society was merely the edge of the psychedelic cosmos, and the conclusion that LSD was the most powerful of these compounds I realised was really not well-founded. What is happening with these tryptamine hallucinogens is a tremendous activation of the visual cortex so that they are true hallucination-inducing drugs. The dominant motif is a flood of visual imagery that, try as one might, one cannot recognise either as the contents of the personal or the collective unconscious. This was truly fascinating to me. I had made a thorough study of Jung and therefore had the expectation that motif and idea systems from the unconscious mind would prove to be reasonably homogeneous world-wide. What I found, instead, with the peak intoxications from these plants, was a world of ideas, visual images and noetic insight that really could not be co-mapped onto any tradition — even the esoteric tradition. All this seemed to go beyond it. This was so fascinating to me that I have made it the compass of my life.

What impact have psychedelics had, in a creative sense, on western culture?
In the West the original contact with altered states of consciousness of any consequence would have to be opium. And opium was a major driving force on the Romantic imagination — Coleridge, De Quincy, Laurence Sterne and a number of other writers were creating a world of darkened ruins, abandoned priories, black waves and desolate shores — clearly a gloss on the opium state. Then around 1820, Byron, Shelley and others began experimenting with hashish as well. But strangely enough, presumably for cultural reasons, hashish never made inroads into the English literary imagination the way opium had. It was left to an American — Fitz Hugh Ludlow — to detail his experiences as an undergraduate at Yale University in 1853, eating large amounts of cannabis jelly. And comporting himself in a way that would be unknown until a hundred years later!

There would come to be a fascination with what Baudelaire and Gautier called the 'artificial Paradise' — they saw these drugs as a tremendous sparkplug to the literary imagination. That attitude was then passed on to people like Havelock Ellis, William James and the Germans Klüver and Lewin, in the matter of mescaline, which was the next compound to be isolated. In the late 1890s Lewin took peyote buttons to Germany and the pure substance was extracted. And there it was pretty much left until the LSD days of the 1960s.

Now, what all these early researchers established, when research was legal, was that these things did create floods of eidetic imagery, they did seem to open up insight into what would have to be called 'mystical landscapes'. There was the sense that they were penetrating into the world of Gnosis.

When LSD was made illegal in the United States in the 1960s, as an afterthought so were all other known psychedelics. And consequently our description of what these things are capable of tends to be equated with a type of instant psychoanalysis. You would take these com-

157

pounds and through a recovery of childhood trauma and insight into your situation you would shed yourself of neurotic attitudes. It was a type of wonder drug for psychological problems. And there it was left, because research became illegal — particularly research with human beings.

Nevertheless, there was a large underground community that continued to dabble in this area and that community began to build up a picture of the activity of these things that went well beyond the Freudian or the Jungian models. What gave particular impetus to this evolving point of view were the experiences people were having with psilocybin. Psilocybin is the active hallucinogenic compound in certain species of mushrooms that have been used for millennia in the central Mexican highlands. Under the influence of psilocybin there is an experience of contacting a speaking entity — an interiorised voice that I call the *Logos*. If we don't go back to Hellenistic Greek terminology then we are left with only the vocabulary of psychopathology. In modern times to hear 'voices' is to be seriously deviant: there is no other way to deal with this. And yet if we go back to the Classical literature the whole goal of Hellenistic esotericism was to gain access to this thing called the *Logos*. The Logos spoke the Truth — an incontrovertible Truth. Socrates had what he called his *daimon* — his informing 'Other'. And the ease with which psilocybin induces this phenomenon makes it, from the viewpoint of a materialist or reductionist rooted in the scientific tradition, almost miraculous.

So I set out to study this phenomenon and to try and determine for myself: was this a deeper level of the psyche that could appear, somehow autonomously, to be a resident 'Other' in the mind with whom one could have conversations? Was this the voice of Mother Nature? Or was it an extra-terrestrial intelligence? These may seem like wild hypotheses but you have to understand that I was pushed to them by *evidence*, by *experience*. This was not 'blue sky' stuff. Here we had a 'voice in the head' eager to reveal vast scenarios of esoteric history, vast millennial unfoldings of the human future.

What did you make of it all?
Well, I still don't have the answer. I vacillate. It depends how close you are to actually having had the experience. While you are having the experience, it is hair-raisingly like dealing with an extra-terrestrial! And yet once you put the experience behind you your rational habits reassert themselves and you say to yourself 'Surely it couldn't have been that . . .'

You feel, don't you, that you are accessing quite different spiritual realms from those described by mystics and gurus from the Eastern traditions?
Yes. Their stress on energy centres in the body, levels of consciousness, the moral perfection of spiritual dimensions — none of this I found to be reliable. What the psilocybin experience seems to argue is that there is a kind of parallel universe that is not at all like our universe and yet it is inhabited by beings with an intentionality. It is not recognisably the universe of astral travel or the Robert Monroe out-of-the-body experiments. What has always put me off about occultists is the humdrum nature of the other world. They talk about radiant people in flowing gowns — ascended masters and so on. My overwhelming impression of the other realm is its utter strangeness — its 'otherness'. It is not even a universe of three dimensional space and time. The other thing about it, which the esoteric traditions to my mind never confront directly, is the reality of it. I am not an occultist. I am spiritual only to the degree that I have been forced to be, by experience. I came into it a reductionist, a rationalist, a materialist, an empiricist — and I say no reductionist, no empiricist could experience what I have experienced without having to seriously re-tool their philosophy. This is not a reality for the menopausal mystic, the self-hypnotised or the soft-headed. This is *real*. And the feeling that radiates out of the psychedelic experience is that it has an historical implication, that what has really happened in the 20th century is that the cataloguing of Nature that began in the 16th century with Linnaeus has at last reached its culmination. And the cataloguing of Nature has revealed things that were totally unexpected, for example, the existence of this potential dimension which our entire language set, emotional set and religious ontology deny. So that what has happened in the 20th century is that we have found out what the witch-doctors are really doing, what the shaman really intends. This information cannot simply be placed in our museums and forgotten: it contains within it a nugget of incontrovertible experience that appears to argue that our vision of reality is sorely lacking. That somehow we have gone down a road of development that has hidden from us vast regions of reality — areas that we have originally dismissed as superstition and now don't mention at all.

Do you feel that the shamanic reality is now the broadest paradigm available to us? Is it broader, say, than the Eastern mystical model?
Oh, yes, I think so. What I think happened is that in the world of pre-history all religion was experiential and it was based on the pursuit of

ecstasy through plants. And at some time, very early, a group inter-posed itself between people and the direct experience of the 'Other'. This created hierarchies, priesthoods, theological systems, castes, ritu-als, taboos. Shamanism, on the other hand, is an experiential science which deals with an area where we know nothing. It is important to remember that our epistemological tools have developed very unevenly in the West. We know a tremendous amount about what is going on in the heart of the atom but we know absolutely nothing about the nature of mind. We haven't a clue. If mathematical formulation is to be the bedrock of ideological certitude then we have no certitude whatsoever in the realm of what is the mind. We *assume* all kinds of things unconsciously but, when pressed, we can't defend our posi-tion.

I think what has happened — because of psychedelics on one level and quantum physics on another — is that the programme of ration-ally understanding Nature has at last been pushed so far that we have reached the irrational core of Nature herself. Now we can see: My God, the tools which brought us here are utterly inadequate.

Is the Human Potential Movement currently re-evaluating the role of psychedelics in understanding the nature of consciousness? Or do you find yourself somewhat out on a limb among your contemporaries?
Well, it's a little of both. The Human Potential Movement at times seems like a flight from the psychedelic experience. It will do any-thing provided there can be certain confidence that it won't work. Therapies like Rolfing have their place but they are not addressing the question: What is the ground of Being?

I am not alone in advocating a revisioning of psychedelics but my colleagues and I certainly represent a highly suspect and not entirely integrated faction of the Human Potential Movement. In a way, you see, we are still reacting to what happened in the 1960s. One can say many things about one's personal psychedelic experiences — and they are always very personal — but if you try to look at 10,000 psych-edelic experiences the generalised conclusion you reach about what these things do is: number one, they dissolve boundaries *whatever the boundaries are*. And as a consequence of this they dissolve cultural programming. They are very democratic — they dissolve all cultural programming. So Marxist, shaman, fundamentalist Christian and nu-clear physicist will all find themselves deeply questioning their own beliefs, post-psychedelic. The thing about LSD which did mark it as different from all the psychedelics was that a reasonably competent chemist could produce 5 million doses in a single day! Well, that was unique in human history. When you go to the Amazon or when you take peyote with the Huichol it is quite a chore to get sufficient material for 20 people. So the release of so much LSD into modern society caused the powers-that-be to assume that the whole social machine was being dissolved in acid — literally, before their very eyes. I think that this was a mistake, to go at it like this. There were many voices at that time, with many theories of how it should be handled. If Aldous Huxley had lived another ten years, it would have been very different. His idea was to get this thing to artists, philosophers, city planners, architects — not every 18 year-old on Earth.

You focus especially on the tryptamines — but is there a cultural factor involved here also? Does a modern-day westerner using these psychedelics access the same reality with these substances as a traditional South American shaman?
Ultimately, I don't think it is cultural. When you smoke DMT you have an experience which comes from the flesh and the bone of your humanness. However, this experience exists entirely as a private reality until you pour it into a linguistic vessel. If you pour it into the linguistic vessel of English, it's going to look very different to the linguistic vessel of Mazatecan. And this has to do with the inevitable relativity of language. So part of what I've done is try to create a phenomenological description of what actually happens. The other thing about these psychedelic experiences is that they are so extraordinary that we have no way to anchor them in memory. If you visit a city you haven't been to before you can always relate it to cities you have been to, but when you go to a place which has no co-mappable points, then you have to create a new language almost from scratch.

Paradoxically, DMT seems to be about the language-forming activity in human beings. Interestingly, some tens of millennia ago the African continent underwent a period of desiccation which continues into the present. And the great rainforests which covered most of Africa began to retreat, leaving grasslands behind them. The primate populations that were arboreal were forced by selective pressure to descend into the grasslands and to abandon their previously vegetarian habits for an omnivorous diet. They already had a complex system of pack signals, as monkeys do, but when they began to develop their hunting strategies on the veldt, there was even more pressure to accelerate and develop this signalling ability. Well, their omnivorous diet led them to focus on the great herds of ungulate animals — wild cattle — that were evolving co-simultaneously. Now in the dung of these ungulate animals the psilocybin mushrooms make their natural home. They are 'coprophilic' that is to say, 'dung-loving' mushrooms. This is the only place they grow. I myself have observed the foraging habits of baboons in Kenya. Baboons scrabble around in the dirt, and one of their favourite tricks is to flip over cow-pies looking for beetles and grubs. So the cow-pie occupies an important position in their world. And yet the mushroom is a totally anomalous object in the veldt environment — it stands out like a sore thumb.

Roland Fischer, who did a lot of work with psilocybin before it became illegal to give it to human beings, made a very interesting observation in the early 1960s. He gave very low doses to people — doses so low that you would not have a psychedelic experience and in fact you would not notice anything much at all, except a slight arousal. But he gave these people visual acuity tests and he discovered that on small doses of psilocybin you can actually see more clearly than in your normal state. You don't have to be an evolutionary biologist to understand that if there is a plant in the environment which confers increased visual acuity on an animal which has a hunting lifestyle, then those animals which accept this item into their diet are going to be more successful hunting and therefore have a more successful reproductive strategy than those animals not admitting the item into their diet. Well, if you take slightly higher doses of psilocybin this restless arousal turns into sexual arousal. And again, more successful copulations mean more successful impregnation, more successful births. This again favours those using the item in their breeding strategy. If you double the dose that causes this sexual arousal you then have a fully fledged contact with something so bizarre, so mysterious, that to this day, 50,000 years later, we still do not have the intellectual equipment to understand it. It appears in the minds of modern human beings with the same transcendental, awe-inspiring force that it must have aroused in the mind of an Australopithecine.

What then is your answer to people who continue to dismiss psychedelic experience as artificial? Surely your view is the exact reverse of that?
Well, there's nothing artificial about it. These things were part of the human food chain from the very beginning. Where the misunderstanding comes is with the label — these are 'drugs' and 'drug' is a red-flag word. We are hysterical over the subject of drugs. Our whole society seems to be dissolving under the onslaught of criminally syndicated drug distribution systems. What we are going to have to do if

we are to come to terms with this is become a little more sophisticated in our definitions. I believe that what we really object to about 'drugs' is that we are alarmed by unexamined, obsessive, self-destructive behaviour. When we see someone acting in this way we draw back. That is what addiction to a drug such as cocaine or morphine results in. However, psychedelics actually *break* habits and patterns of thought. They actually cause individuals to inspect the structure of their lives and make judgements about it. Now, what psychedelics share with 'drugs' is that they are physical compounds, often pressed into pills, and you do put them into your body. But I believe that a reasonable definition of drugs would have us legalise psilocybin and outlaw television! Imagine if the Japanese had won World War II and had introduced into American life a drug so insidious that, 30 years later, the average American was spending five hours a day 'loaded' on this drug. People would just view it as the most outrageous atrocity ever. And yet, we in America do this to ourselves. And the horrifying thing about the 'trip' which television gives you is that it's not your trip. It is a trip which comes down through the value systems of a society whose greatest god is the almighty dollar. So television *is* the opiate of the people. I think the tremendous governmental resistance to the psychedelic issue is not because psychedelics are multi-million dollar criminal enterprises — they are trivial on that level. However, they inspire examination of values, and that is the most corrosive thing that can happen.

Your idea is of the psychedelic pioneer as a type of alchemist who can make the soul tangible, as it were. Could you tell us more about this?
Alchemy was the belief that spirit somehow resided at the heart of matter. The alchemists were the heirs to the great Hellenistic religious systems that are generally tagged as 'Gnostic'. The central idea of Gnosticism is that the material of which 'soul' and true 'being' is composed is trapped through a series of cosmic misfortunes in a low-level universe that is alien to it. And the alchemists literalised these ideas to suggest that the spirit could somehow be distilled, or coaxed from the dense matrix of matter. Well, this is also what the psychedelics reinforce and it is interesting to see how alchemists at different times have contributed to the advancement of pharmacology. For instance, distilled alcohol was discovered by alchemists seeking the elixir of life, and Paracelsus popularised opium. This is not to fault the alchemical quest but to show that alchemy — the belief that there is spirit in matter — was a survival of an older, shamanic strata of belief which

involved gaining the alliance of a plant. The notion that one can do it by oneself, I think, is preposterous. It is virtually impossible to have the spiritual experiences which confirm a certain moral order and value system unless you resort to psychedelics or alternatively, fasting or getting lost in the wilderness. I don't think people realise quite how efficacious the psychedelics are — these things work!

I just wish people could be more catholic in their tastes. I mean, if you are an advocate of the virtues of yoga or natural diet or mantras — you really owe it to yourself to explore them using psychedelics at the same time. I explored the possibilities I have just mentioned before settling on the golden road to the soul.

So why is there such tremendous prejudice, both in the East and the West, against psychedelics?
I think people are in love with the journey. People love seeking answers. If you were to suggest to people that the time of seeking is over and that the chore is now to face the answer, that's more of a challenge! Anyone can sweep up around the ashram for 12 years while congratulating themselves that they are following Baba into enlightenment. It takes courage to take psychedelics, *real courage!* Your stomach clenches, your palms grow damp, because you realise this is real — this is going to work. Not in 12 years, not in 20 years, but in an hour! What I see in the whole spiritual enterprise is a great number of people supporting themselves in one way or another on the basis of their lack of success. Were they ever to succeed, these enterprises would all be put out of business. No-one's in a hurry for that!

In your scheme of things, is there any place for institutionalised religion, for orthodox religious beliefs?
Yes. What I have found is that all of these systems which are offered as spiritual paths work splendidly in the presence of psychedelics. If you think mantras are effective, try a mantra on 20 milligrams of psilocybin and see what happens. All sincere religious motivation is illuminated by psychedelics. To put it perhaps in a trivial way, the religious quest is an automobile but psychedelics are the petrol which runs it! You go nowhere without the fuel no matter how finely crafted the upholstery, how flawlessly machined the engine.

Where do you personally think the Human Potential Movement is heading now and where do you position yourself in that spectrum?
I believe that the best idea will win. We are all under an obligation to ourselves and to the world to do our best — to place the best ideas on

the table. Then all we have to do is stand back and watch. I have this Darwinian belief that the correct idea will emerge triumphant. To my way of thinking psychedelics provide the only category which is authentic enough to be legislated out of existence. They're not going to make Rolfing or wheat grass juice illegal — these things pose no problem. But I think we're going to have to come to terms with the psychedelic possibility. We would have a long time ago in America except for the fact that, on this issue, the Government acts as the enforcing arm of Christian fundamentalism. Life, liberty and the pursuit of happiness are enshrined in the Constitution of the United States as *inalienable rights*. Well, if the pursuit of happiness does not cover the psychedelic quest for enlightenment, then I don't know what that can mean. I think we are headed for a darker period before the light, because the self-deceiving cant of the Government on the issue is going to have to be exposed for what it is. I see the whole 'hard drug' thing as an enormous con-game. Governments have always been the major purveyors of addictive drugs — right back to the sugar trade in England, the opium wars in China, the CIA's involvement in the heroin trade in South-East Asia during the 1960s and the current cocaine distribution coming out of South America. We're going to have to abandon this Christian wish to legislate other people's behaviour 'for their own good'. Let's take two drugs for a moment, and contrast them: Cocaine is ultra-chic, costs $150 per gram, is utterly worthless as far as I can see, and doesn't get you as stoned as a double espresso. Then there's airplane glue. It costs $1.20 a tube, you can totally waste yourself with it, and probably kill yourself no faster than you can with cocaine. So why aren't people in Dior gowns, driving Rolls Royces, honking up airplane glue? Because it's tatty, grotesque, *declassé*. And this is what we have to put across about these hard drugs. The only way you can do that is to reduce the price of cocaine to $1.25 a gram. Then it will be seen as a horrible, banal, destructive thing. Only when Governments intervene by restricting access do things suddenly gain this astronomical worth. So it's a game that the Government is playing.

I do see signs in a number of countries that Governments are at last heeding the environmental message. If we consider the concept of the Gaia Hypothesis as a reflection of an emerging global awareness, it also seems to me that your concept of the 'Oversoul' of the planet could also become important . . .

These things are all part of the 'New Age' but I have abandoned that term in favour of what I call the Archaic Revival — which places it all

165

in a better historical perspective. When a culture loses its bearings, the traditional response is to go back in history to find the previous 'anchoring' model. An example of this would be the breakup of the medieval world at the time of the Renaissance. They had lost their compass so they went back to Greek and Roman models and created Classicism — Roman law, Greek aesthetics and so on.

In the 20th century a global civilisation has lost its bearings and as we look back in time for a model to anchor us we have to go back before history to around 12 or 15 thousand years ago. So the important part of the Human Potential Movement and the New Age, I believe, is the re-empowerment of ritual, the rediscovery of shamanism, the recognition of psychedelics and the importance of the Goddess. There must also be an authentic religious mystery driving this. Psychedelics put you in touch with something that is both real and immediate — the mind of the planet. This is the Oversoul of all life on Earth. It's the real thing. The Gaia Hypothesis which began by proposing that the entire planet is a self-regulating system has now been brought to the level where some people are saying 'It's almost alive . . .'. But I would go much further than that. Not only is it alive, but 'minded'.

I take very seriously the idea that the Logos is real, that there is a guiding Mind — an Oversoul — that inhabits the biome of the planet, and that human balance, dignity and religiosity depend on having direct contract with this realm. That's what shamanism is providing. It was available in the West until the fall of Eleusis and the Mystery traditions — to some people — but then it was stamped out by barbarians who didn't realise what they had destroyed.

The soul of the planet is not neutral about the emerging direction of human history. We are part of a cosmic drama — I really believe that — and although the cosmic drama has lasted for untold ages, I don't think it's going to run for untold ages into the future.

You see all this reaching some sort of climax in 2012 AD. Could you explain that?
I see some sort of culmination in 2012. The Mayans also set 2012 as the end of 5,128-year cycle. I believe that what we call historical existence is a self-limiting situation that cannot be projected centuries into the future. We are tearing the Earth to pieces, we are spewing out toxins — and the entire planet is reacting. Psychedelics are going to play a major role in helping people to become aware of what is *really* happening.

You have said that an important part of the mystical quest is to face up to death and recognise it as a rhythm of life. Would you like to enlarge on your views on the implications of the dying process?

I take seriously the notion that these psychedelic states are anticipations of the dying process — or, as the Tibetans refer to them, the Bardo levels beyond death. It seems likely that our physical lives are a type of launching-pad for the soul. As the esoteric traditions say, life is an opportunity to prepare for death and we should learn to recognise the signposts along the way, so that when death comes, we can make the transition smoothly. I think the psychedelics show you the transcendental nature of reality. It would be hard to die gracefully as an atheist or existentialist. Why should you? Why not rage against the dying of the light? But if in fact this is not the dying of the light but the Dawning of the Great Light, then one should certainly not rage against that. There's a tendency in the New Age to deny death. We have people pursuing physical immortality and freezing their heads until the fifth millennium, when they can be thawed out. All of this indicates a lack of balance or equilibrium. The Tao flows through the realms of life and non-life with equal ease.

Do you personally regard the death process as a journey into one's own belief system?

Like the psychedelic experience, death must be poured into the vessel of language. But dying is essentially physiological. It may be that there are certain compounds in the brain that are only released when it is impossible to reverse the dying process. And yet the near death experience has a curious affinity to the shamanic voyage and the psychedelic experience.

I believe that the best map we have of consciousness is the shamanic map. According to this viewpoint, the world has a 'centre' and when you go to the centre — which is inside yourself — there is a vertical axis which allows you to travel up or down. There are celestial worlds, there are infernal worlds, there are paradisiacal worlds. These are the worlds that open up to us on our shamanic journeys and I feel we have an obligation to explore these domains and pass on that information to others interested in mapping the psyche. At this time in our history, it's perhaps the most awe-inspiring journey anyone could hope to make!

10
Computers, Consciousness and Creativity :
An Interview with Dr Timothy Leary

During the late 1960s, depending on your viewpoint, Dr Timothy Leary was either a villain or a hero. Associated with the Hippie movement and popular interest in psychedelics, the former Harvard University psychologist became famous for his slogan 'Turn on, tune in , drop out' proclaimed at the 'Love-In' in San Francisco's Golden Gate Park in 1967. President Nixon called him 'the most dangerous man alive' and for a time he became a political scapegoat, arrested by G. Gordon Liddy and jailed on two occasions — in 1965 and 1970 — for possessing a small quantity of marijuana.

Since 1980, however, Dr Leary has made something of a comeback, lecturing, writing, consulting and designing computer software for the 21st Century. His controversial autobiography, *Flashbacks*, was published in 1983 and helped to bring his extraordinary career into some sort of perspective.[1]

Those who have categorised Leary simply as a figure of the 1960s counter-culture do him an injustice, for he has kept well ahead of trends in the Human Potential Movement. His mind remains as sharp as ever, his vision for the future crystal clear. He is now President of an electronic research and development group called Futique Inc., which specialises in multi-media education packages involving the collaboration of computer programmers, psychologists, writers, artists, linguists and musicians.

Could you describe the computer products you are promoting — what are they and what do they do?
What I'm doing here is something I've been working on since 1946, when I first started my research doctorate at the University of California in Berkeley. Basically, I'm setting up communications methods for people — young and old — to help them communicate with au-

168

thorities, teachers, administrators and parents. Right now I'm working on a series of software programmes which utilise the computer as a method for electronic learning and electronic mind-communication. So I to try to find people interested in working with my software. I'm not selling it, I'm giving out versions, or models, that people can use in their classrooms, or in their writing or their communication. People have to send back copies of their discs so we can see what improvements they have made.

In all of our software programmes the teacher can pitch a notion and then the student answers it and scores their own response. The questions presented by the teacher are in one of four modes : the teacher can be pedantic, comic, bureaucratic or imaginative. In every mode the teacher can also lie, but as in cricket or baseball, the bowler is supposed to test your skill and it is up to the student to react to the different modes. The student learns to detect the lie, to test his own capacity to bluff, to be gullible or timid. The student may also be asked to be comic in his response, or to be dull and bureaucratic, or creative and imaginative. Instead of just producing one answer, one way to respond, and one 'true or false', the student learns meta-creativity. He learns how to be dumb, how to be funny, how to be precise, how to be fuzzy — it all has to do with improving communication and thinking. In all of our programmes, once all the scoring has been done, the student can appeal and can change his own score. But it's all a type of feedback. There's no teacher judging you, there's no giving out scores like the great Biblical prosecutor in the sky. In most of our programmes, at the end, the student scores the teacher — on how creative the process has been and the teacher is able to react to the student. In other words, we are turning the hierarchical educational system into a fast-moving game of mental ping-pong or mental chess, in which the teacher becomes an interactor. The student learns from the teacher and the teacher learns from the student.

Education is the number one problem in the USA today, so we are trying to nurture creativity. That sounds like a cliche, but you have to have quick feedback of response. Our programmes help people to think for themselves in a way which needs to be creative.

Are the software programmes self-contained, enabling people to work by themselves ?
Some of the programmes you can buy in software stores or by mail order. However, many of them we are circulating in experimental form and we will eventually be publishing electronic texts geared to

nurturing creativity. With the average school text, the student buys it and the job, more or less, is to learn in rote form what's in it. Our texts are bedded in quick feedback programmes to sponsor creativity so we're not interested in your ability as a student to regurgitate everything that is in the text. We want the student to become extremely creative. Students tend to learn and remember three or four times the amount of material when they are active and creative, so in fact the two things tend to go together.

I understand you are also involved with revolutionary forms of computer clothing, or cyberware, designed to stimulate creativity ?
This is the hottest new field in American software. The concept involves an 'artificial reality' where you create and design cybernetic realities on a screen by digitising photographs. You can digitise a photograph of yourself, your home, your office or your vacation spot. Then you put on goggles which have television lenses in them. This equipment enables you to walk around inside the cybernetic environment you have created. Say you are watching the 7 o'clock news. Well, that can be taped and any section you want to change can be overlaid with any other digitised graphic. You can walk up to a President or Prime Minister, change their voices, make your own programmes, and so on.

In about five years there will be comparatively inexpensive forms of computer clothing. These will employ twelve pressure points in the body that you articulate to allow you to make authentic movements on a screen. Let's say you want to dial a person and 'meet' for a conference. That person can be in Tokyo or New York but you can decide where you meet — your place or his, or on the top of Mount Everest or Acapulco Beach. You simply go through your file and pull out that location. This means you can design and control your realities. You have to learn how to use your arms and legs on the screen — you gradually become more proficient at this.

But how real is the conversation that happens between these two people ?
It's as real as a telephone conversation. Everything I'm talking about now is like a telephone except that instead of just phonetics it provides visuals.

What about when I call President Clinton and he doesn't know I'm calling him ?
That's a different situation. The first application, as I said, is like the telephone. The second version involves tapes, and we have that tech-

nology already — like when you call up an airline and get a taped recorded message. Of course, that's not interactive. However, you can take such information that's digitised and put it into your computer. Then you can play parts in the great movies! You can be Clarke Gable in *Gone With The Wind*. You can make your own news . . .

So this is where the stimulus to the imagination comes in ?
Totally. Anything you can visualise, hallucinate or dream up — things that you can't do in Newtonian three-dimensional reality — all of these fantasies can become tangible. We are talking here about the basic technique, often used in business, of simulation : 'What if . . .? *What if* we make the budget larger, *what if* we cut prices, *what if* we make the struts ten degrees stronger? Engineers use this approach all the time. Word processors and spread sheets also do it. The computer is wonderful for the simulation mode. It does all the leg-work. Everything we are doing with a computer could of course be done by human beings but it would take so long.

There seems to be an important difference, though, between the psychedelic experience and computer-created realities, however imaginative. With psychedelics one is able to access material that was previously unconscious — including archetypal imagery, mythic symbols and even 'cellular' consciousness. With the computer systems, the conscious self is the starting point and you have to be able to visualise the parameters you wish to explore with the computer. There is no capacity for unleashing the unconscious, as it were. So isn't the psychedelic experience a much bigger concept than what you are exploring here with computers?
What we call the psychedelic experience is, of course, just the brain with the conditioned programming diminished or pulled out. The brain processes 125 million signals per second, so there's a lot of show-biz going on inside the brain. In the psychedelic or visionary experience the brain operates using algorithms which are much more complex, but essentially similar, to those used by a computer. All through history, mystics and visionaries have come back from their experiences saying " "Wow, it's ineffable — you can't put it into words." Of course you can't put it into words. Words are just lumbering along at two or three a second and your brain is pouring out at 125 million a second. Great artists occasionally have come back from their voyages within with `still shots' or `snap shots' as it were. Hieronymus Bosch is one who comes to mind. The great visionary musicians and film-makers all have the ability to make explicit some of the wonder and

171

complexity of the inner panorama.

What is the connection between consciousness and the brain?

In the brain you are talking about 100 billion neurons and each neuron, we now realise, has the communicating and processing potential of a big computer. So you are talking about a situation where the entire universe could be dealt with by your brain. As a matter of fact, the actual physical universe probably isn't as complicated as the brain. And the brain isn't as complicated as the DNA code which is present in every cell in your body and provides the conscious intelligence that creates the brain. We are talking here about invisible miniaturised informational processes of increasing power. The paradox in the cybernetic, psychedelic or 'spiritual' worlds is that the smaller the manifested form, the more information is contained within it. Now we realise that inside an atom there is probably more information than in a molecule. The quark — which is only a single unit — contains more information than an Amazon forest! All matter and energy in the universe is just frozen information.

What is so intriguing about our own era in history is that the human quest for knowledge and understanding in the last 25 years has seen an amazing blend of shamanic techniques, psychedelic drugs and the international global boom in resurrecting the pre-Christian, pagan, totemic and Hindu traditions. At the same time, with these computers you wear you have a situation where you can walk around in realities of your own construction. So we are very much on a threshold. I don't want to put any limits on what I'm saying but here we have ancient techniques merging with the most modern. Computers give us the ways to communicate with the basic language of the universe — which is *quanta-electronic*. Matter and bodies are just electrons that have decided to come together, buzzing around with information. Medieval alchemy made this point in the dictum 'dissolve and coagulate'. Dissolve the big structures into smaller units and then they'll rejoin into something better . . .

So, without being too simplistic about it, do you see the universe as a blaze of information, an electronic pulse ?

The current version of the universe which makes most sense to me is the model based on Quantum Physics and Einstein's Relativity, which proposes that there is no absolute space or time, just 'fields'. I'm changing, you're changing. And the only way to understand who I am and who you are is to get feedback, to keep in touch.

But then there's a point at which the boundary of 'you' and the boundary of 'me' disappears and maybe we perceive each other as being the same energy at a core level . . . ?
Hinduism and Buddhism are now being approached by Quantum physicists in exactly the way you are suggesting. Of course, the concept of 'you' and 'me' is changing anyway. Every seven days all the atoms in our bodies change over.

As you look back on the 1960s, what do you think are the most important lessons or insights for our society which have emerged from that time ?
A precious natural resource, as we lurch into the 21st Century — far beyond the value of oil or metal — is human creativity. Throughout history, in the feudal and industrial ages, creativity has been deliberately held down by every educational, every religious, and almost every political organisation. With too much creativity you can't get the job done. You need a lot of conformity, an assembly line and a mechanical approach, and there's nothing wrong with that. Until you get to a certain level of experience as a species you can't think for yourself. But our species is now reaching a level of maturity where everyone has got to be creative and innovative, and the main job of society is to help us do that. It should be a function of schools not to indoctrinate and teach kids how to conform but to foster creativity.

But obviously there are lots of people who have a vested interest in maintaining the status quo. Do you think the world will increasingly polarise into those embracing the information age of the future versus those clinging desperately to vestiges of the past ?
There will probably be localisations in different countries. We're trying to introduce our software into schools but every single school board in the world — communist, Catholic, whatever — is against any change for the obvious reasons. So there will be certain suburbs or neighbourhoods in Sydney, for example, which are open-minded, and which will communicate with people in Princeton, New Jersey. There will be little pockets of people, like beacons or lighthouses, which will stand out and emerge into networks. However the majority of the human race at any one time doesn't want to change that much. Fortunately the children will want to. In the next ten years we will see at least a doubling in human intelligence.

Do you see the 1960s as the time when we first began to break out of the

mould as a western civilisation, and to escape from routine thinking ?
As a mass, certainly. What started in the '60s really began in the '50s.
World War Two was the final war — a glorious orgasmic end to industrial imperialism — because everyone knew that you couldn't have
another one after Hiroshima and Nagasaki. Then what happened was
during the 1950s the children in the western civilisations began watching television and, for the first time, twenty or thirty million children
watching *The Mouseketeers* were all singing the same song at the same
time. Now that was a new species, turning on and tuning in . . .

In the 1950s the medium was television, but then in the 1960s people realised they could do the same thing with their brains. This was
the consciousness revolution known as the psychedelic era. You can't
overemphasise the importance of the '60s for the personal, individual,
transpersonal and religious — it comes up in many ways. Amongst us
right now there are millions — tens of millions — who have made that
leap of understanding. So, in the 1950s it was passive, a matter of
watching television, and in the 1960s and 1970s it was active exploring
your own potential, either with or without drugs. Now, in the 1990s
it is going to be the era of computer software used as tools for creativity. The human being is going to transcend the limitations of space
and time. We have to break down the barriers of the walls of the
classroom. People will be studying the same subjects together but the
classroom will be an electronic classroom. It will also be a matter of
breaking down the barriers of nationalism. That's already beginning
to happen with fax machines and telephones. So the Hindu concept
that 'We're all one' is going to come true!

Footnotes

Chapter 1: The Magical Universe

1. The accounts of Carlos Castaneda have been questioned by Richard de Mille in *Castaneda's Journey* (1976), but at the time of writing Castaneda had not responded to de Mille's charge that Don Juan was an imaginary concoction. There seems to be general agreement that the themes of Castaneda's books are authentic, whether or not they are borrowed from other anthropological sources.
2. See R. Hughes, *Heaven and Hell in Western Art*, p.22.
3. G. Chevalier, *The Sacred Magician*, p.95.
4. Ibid., p.96.
5. F. Bardon, *The Practice of Magical Evocation*, p.59.
6. Ibid., p.125.
7. Ibid., p.126.
8. Ibid., p.19.
9. See Edward F. Heenan, *Mystery, Magic and Miracle*, p.85, and I. Zaretsky and M. Leone, *Religious Movements in ContemporaryAmerica*, p.663.
10. S. Arieti, *Creativity, p.22 1.*
11. *777* is included in A. Crowley, *The Qabalah of Aleister Crowley*, an anthology of major magical writings.
12. A. Crowley, *The Qabalah of Aleister Crowley*, introduction by Israel Regardie.
13. G. Scholem, *Kabbalah, p.203.*
14. H. Zimmer, *The King and the Corpse*, p.178.

Chapter 2: Archetypes and Belief Systems

1. C. G. Jung, *The Integration of the Personality*, p.89.
2. I. Regardie, *The Art and Meaning of Magic*, p.13.
3. C. G. Jung, 'The Structure of the Psyche' in *The Structure and Dynamics of the Psyche*, p.158.
4. W. E. Butler, *Magic, its Ritual Power and Purpose*, pp.17-18.
5. J. Jacobi, *The Psychology of C. G. Jung*, pp.47-48.
6. E. Edinger, *Ego and Archetype, p.96.*
7. W. E. Butler, op. cit., p.16.
8. D. Fortune, *The Mystical Qabalah*, pp.10-11.
9. J. Jacobi, op. cit., p.94.
10. Ibid., p.139.

11. Ibid., p.152.
12. See especially E. Howe, *The Magicians of the Golden Dawn*, referred to in Chapter 1.
13. J. Lilly, *Simulations of God*, p.84.
14. See especiallv M. Eliade, *Cosmos and History*.
15. J. Lilly, op. cit., pp.146-7.
16. See M. Eliade, *Shamanism*, p.42.
17. S. Arieti, *Creativity*.
18. J. Lilly, *The Dyadic Cyclone*, Chapter 12.

Chapter 3: The Tarot and Transformation

1. This concept is an integral part of modern magical thought and is central to the definitions of magic proposed by Dion Fortune and Aleister Crowley.
2. For a description of early theories concerning Tarot origins see S. Kaplan, *Tarot Classic*.
3. F. King, *Astral Projection, Magic and Alchemy*.
4. Ibid., pp.84-5.
5. R. Cavendish, *The Tarot*, p.146.
6. The Qlippoth are the 'negative' sephiroth which constitute the black Tree — the polar opposite of the transcendental shamanistic framework.
7. D. Miller, *The New Polytheism*, p.55.
8. Chakras are hypothetical energy centres in man, usually associated with the central nervous system.

Chapter 4: Surrealism and the Qabalah

1. A. Balakian, *Surrealism: The Road to the Absolute*, p.128.
2. J. Russell, *Max Ernst*, p.55.
3. J. H. Matthews, *An introduction to Surrealism*, p.114.
4. Ibid., p.54.
5. Ibid., p.71.
6. M. Jean, *The History of Surrealist Painting*, p.207.
7. P.Waldo-Schwartz, *Art and the Occult*, p.102.
8. D. Sylvester, *Magritte*, p.14.
9. Included in L. Lippard (ed.), *Surrealists on Art*, p.155.
10. C. Castaneda, *The Teachings of Don Juan*, 1968, p.188.
11. Quoted in J. T. Soby, *Magritte*, p.7.
12. M. Jean, op. cit., p.275.
13. J. T. Soby, *Yves Tanguy*, p.18.
14. See L. Lippard, op. cit., p.97.
15. While Laing's writings on the relativity of insanity are well known the extraordinary examination of hallucinatory insanity bv Wilson Van Dusen is less so. Interested readers are referred to Van Dusen's *The Natural Depth in Man*, and his perceptive article 'Hallucinations as the World of Spirits' contained in John White's *Frontiers of Consciousness*.
16. P.Walton, *Dali/Miro*, p.7.
17. Quoted in G. Xuriguera, *Winfredo Lam*, p.23.
18. Ibid., p.9.

19. Ibid., p.23.
20. N. Drury and S. Skinner, *The Search for Abraxas*, pp.49-71,
21. John Russell (1967: p.106) has written that Ernst's birds do not find themselves trapped in the forest and are invariably symbols of transcendence. The sun, mythologically, is the prime symbol of individuation — the spiritual focusing and harmonizing of the life processes.
22. Included in L. Lippard (ed.), op. cit., p.118 et seq.
23. Ibid., p.121.
24. A condensed account of Spare's sigil method is contained in N. Drury and S. Skinner, op. cit., Spare's major magical treatise *The Book Of Pleasure,* which contains his most complete statement on sigils and magical energy, has been reissued Montreal, 1976, 93 Publishing.
25. L. Lippard, op. cit., p.121.
26. M. Ernst, 'What is Surrealism?' in L. Lippard, op. cit., p.134.
27. J. Russell, op. cit., p.50.
28. J. Fadiman and R. Frager, *Personality and Personal Growth,* pp.306,340.

Chapter 5: *The Magic of Austin Spare*

1. Kenneth Grant: *Images and Oracles of Austin Osman Spare*, page 33.
2. Spare defined Kia as 'the absolute freedom which being free is mighty enough to be *reality . . .* '
3. Spare took as his own magical name Zos vel Thanatos.
4. In the Qabalah, the Sephirah or stage of consciousness, Malkuth, which corresponds to the visible universe, is regarded as feminine. (The daughter of Kether, the first emanation.) Robert Graves has shown that Nature is universally venerated, in various forms and guises, as the Great White Goddess.
5. Nakedness symbolises the 'recovered innocence' or 'purity': the state of Adam before the Fall.
6. He was also critical of occultists who, like the Church, claimed to be carrying on a Tradition. This, Spare believed, led by its very nature to a loss of vitality. Kenneth Grant summarises Spare's attitude: 'The ceremonial magician sets his stage for the rehearsal of reality with all the traditional weapons; but Zos (Austin Spare) maintains that this is unnecessary mummery because the apprehension of our greater realities is to be effected consciously through living the symbolic simulations of the ego 'as if' they were real, not a mock rehearsal but as a spontaneous evocation within the magical circle of immediacy-*now*.' (Carfax Monograph IV.) reprinted in Kenneth Grant *Hidden Lore* (see bibliography).
7. This implies a God-like purity of being that few in history would seem to have attained; those who resist the dissolution into the Godhead and choose instead to stay to help mankind by imparting their wisdom are known as avatars. They assume Divine incarnations of the status of a Buddha or a Christ, for example.
8. This had been preceded by *A Book of Satyrs* (c. 1911) which contained 'satires' on the Church, politics, officialdom and other 'follies'. It is not a major work.
9. Spare believed that the self lived 'in millions of forms', and that it was

obliged to experience 'every conceivable thing', i. e. all the infinite possibilities inherent in the manifested universe. (They were also inherent in Kia but the self didn't realise that.) Any incomplete existence or situation required a reincarnation to finalise it or make it whole: 'I have incarnated that which I need to rationalise.' Spare also thought that by exploring the inner recesses of the mind one would undoubtedly uncover past incarnations. 'For whatever is attained is but a re-awakening of an earlier experience of the body.'

10. These 'impressions' contained a record of man's eternal past because they were aspects of the total karma, the 'essence of self' which survived each separate existence. Spare soon realized that a great number of these subconscious contents were bestial and his later illustrations show an increasing intermingling between the *actual,* and these thought forms conjured up in *trance.* It is interesting to note that one of the methods employed by occultists is to identify with, and imagine oneself as, a God, e. g. Thoth. It is believed that in so doing, one experiences the qualities of the God and correspondingly one's own spiritual state is modified. The Golden Dawn and A.˙. A.˙. incorporated meditations on the Egyptian pantheon, and it is not surprising, in view of the fact that many of the Gods (Thoth, Horus etc.) have animal heads, that some meditators should have acquired atavistic qualities. Crowley was keen to identify with the Great Beast 666 of *Revelations* and Spare frequently identified with the goat!

11. Note Spare's reference to 'regression'. Most occultists and mystics prefer to consider their methods 'evolutionary'.

12. In order to attract at an inner level a 'true' response, the sigil had to be free of 'superfluous elements', hence its simplification. Otherwise uncalled for results could rebound from the subconscious.

13. This method appears to resemble that of the Whirling Dervishes who induce visions by acts involving extreme physical exhaustion.

14. See Jean Overton Fuller's *The Magical Dilemma of Victor Neuburg.* W. H. Allen, London, 1965

15. This is a well-known technique in 'astral projection'.

16. Spare wrote: 'Man implies Woman. I transcend these by the Hermaphrodite, this again implies a Eunuch', i. e. Man/Woman in the world becomes the Hermaphrodite or Divine Union of the Sexes in Kether which in turn becomes the Eunuch or Non-Sex of Ain Soph/Kia.

17. A similar technique to Tattva visions in traditional Magic.

18. Occultists also believe that astral projection simulates the process of death. In the first instance the consciousness is projected into a vehicle forged by the imagination. In death the vehicle does not return, for the bond with the body is broken.

19. The Zos, according to Spare, needs to discover things about itself and Kia and this is the reason behind reincarnation, as explained earlier.

20. A theory often reiterated by Aleister Crowley.

21. For example, said Spare, one would be able to hear within the mind 'the most transcendental music ever conceived'.

22. In his autobiography, *Memories, Dreams, Reflections,* Dr. Carl Jung warned against the possibility of allowing the symbolic contents of dreams and

visions to be indulged in, rather than checked. Jung believed that the perception of dual, but intermingled, levels of awareness (e. g. atavism and reality) could lead to schizophrenia. One wonders if Spare would agree.

23. In the illustration to this text, thought-forms swirl around a head which is undoubtedly feminine. In light of the fact that the book is titled *The Focus of Life* and contains Spare's own visions, this is rather puzzling. The other illustrations also contain naked (primitive?) women, but no drawing of Spare himself, which is again unusual because in *The Starlit Mire*, Spare shows his own head surrounded by atavisms (The Seven Devils), and a similar drawing occurs in *The Book of Pleasure*. The only plausible reason for Spare's insistence on the feminine form in *The Focus of Lift* is that it may refer to the occult doctrine of the alteration of the sexual polarity on succesive mystical planes.

24. A Gnostified extension of A. O. S., Spare's initials.

25. Aleister Crowley wrote: 'When you have proved that God is merely a name for the sex instinct, it appears to me not far to the perception that the sex instinct is God . . .'

26. John Symonds, *The Great Beast*, Rider and Co., London, 1952, p.11.

Chapter 6: The Supernatural World of Rosaleen Norton

1. For a full account of Rosaleen Norton's trance explorations see N.Drury, *Pan's Daughter: the Magical World of Rosaleen Norton*, Mandrake, Oxford 1993

2. A facsimile of this edition, *The Art of Rosaleen Norton*, was published by Walter Glover in Sydney in 1982

3. See *The Art of Rosaleen Norton*, 1982, p.38

4. Ibid, p.26

Chapter 7 : Beyond the New Age

1. Quoted in Jonathon Adolph: 'What is New Age? And Where is it Going?' *New Age News* Sydney, Vol 2 No 2, May 1988

2. Ibid, p. 13

3. Walden (various editions), Chapter 16

4. Quoted in A. Watson and N. Drury, *Healing Music*, Prism Press, Dorset, 1988, p. 22

5. S. Miller, Dimensions of Humanistic Medicine, quoted in K. Pelletier, *Holistic Health*, Delta Books, New York 1979, p. 35

6. Joan Halifax, *Shamanic Voices*, Dutton, New York, 1979, p. 21

7. James Cowan, *Mysteries of the Dreaming*, Unity Press, Sydney 1989, p. 27

8. *The Awakening Earth*, Ark Books, London 1982, p. 12

9. Ron Boyer, 'The Vision Quest', *The Laughing Man*, Vol 2 No 4, p. 63

10. Ralph Metzner, 'Gaia's Alchemy' in Fredric Lehrman, *The Sacred Landscape*, Celestial Arts, Berkeley 1988, p. 119

11. For further information see N & S Drury, *Healing Oils and Essences*, Harper & Row, Sydney 1988

12. *New Age News*, Sydney, Vol 1, No 10, December 1987

13. Lynette Mayblom, 'Planting Crystals', *Southern Crossings*, Sydney, Vol 6

No 1, p. 7, August-September 1985
14. Mark Chipperfield, 'New Age Inc.' *The Australian Magazine*, Sydney, 10 December 1988
15. Ibid
16. Quoted in N. Drury, *Healers, Quacks or Mystics?* Hale & Iremonger, Sydney 1983, p. 45
17. Ibid
18. N. Drury, *The Elements of Human Potential*, Element Books, Dorset 1989, pp. 90-91
19. N. Drury: Interview with Dr Michael Harner in New York, November 1984
20. N. Drury, 'The Shaman: Healer and Visionary', *Nature & Health* Sydney, Vol 9 No 2, p. 86
21. N. Drury, *The Elements of Shamanism*, Element Books, Dorset 1989, p. 98
22. Ibid, p. 99
23. For further information see John C. Lilly, *The Centre of the Cyclone*, Calder & Boyars, London, 1973 and *The Human Biocomputer*, Abacus, London 1974
24. N. Drury, 'The Samadhi Tank Experience', *Nature & Health*, Sydney, Vol 5 No 5, Summer 1984
25. Quoted in N.Drury, *The Occult Experience*, London 1987, Robert Hale, p.44
26. Ibid
27. Quoted in Victoria Williams, 'The Sacred Craft', *East West*, October 1984
28. Mirka Knaster, 'The Goddesses in Jean Shinoda Bolen', *East West*, March 1989, p.45
29. Ibid., p.44
30. Ibid., p.73
31. Jean Houston, 'Myth and Pathos in Sacred Psychology', *Dromenon* Vol.3, No.2, Spring 1981, p.32
32. Ibid., p.33
33. Richard Daab, 'An Interview with Jean Houston', *Magical Blend*, No.18, February/April 1988, p.25
34. Richard Daab, continuation of article on Jean Houston, *Magical Blend*, No.20, August/October 1988, pp. 23-24

Chapter 8: Contemporary Shamanism and the Earth Mother

1. Personal communication, November 19842. Mimi Albert, 'Out of Africa', Jan./Feb. 1987
3. Personal communication, November 1984
4. Mimi Albert, op cit.
5. Michele Jamal, *Shape Shifters*. 1987, p,164
6. Ibid. p.165
7. Ibid. p.164
8. Ibid. p.162
9. Joan Halifax, *Shamanic Voices*, 1979, p.68
10. Ibid. pp.89-90

11. Michele Jamal, op cit. pp.89-90
12. Robert Neubert, 'Sun Bear - Walking in Balance on the Earth Mother',
    p.10
13. Ibid. p.9
14. Sun Bear and Wabun, *The Medicine Wheel*, 1980, p.xiii
15. Ron Boyer, 'The Vision Quest'*The Laughing Man* Vol,2 No.4, p.63
16. Ibid. p.60
17. Ibid. p.61
18. Ibid. P.62

Chapter 9 :Sacred Plants and Mystic Realities
1. For further observations on McKenna's viewpoints see the collection of
   interviews included in T.McKenna, *The Archaic Revival*, Harper Collins,
   San Francisco 1991

Chapter 10 : Computers, Consciousness and Creativity
1. Leary has published previous autobiographical material, including his controversial volume *High Priest* (New York, 1968), but *Flashbacks* remains
   the most coherent overview of his career up to 1983

Bibliography

Chapter 1: The magical universe

Arieti, S., *Creativity: the Magical Synthesis,* New York, 1976, Basic Books Inc.

Bardon, F., *Initiation into Hermetics,* Koblenz, 1962, Osiris Verlag.

Bardon, F., *The Practice of Magical Evocation,* Graz, 1967, Rudolph Pravica.

Barrett, F., *The Magus,* New York, 1973, University Books/Citadel.

Chevalier, G., *The Sacred Magician,* London, 1976, Paladin.

Colquhoun, I., *Sword of Wisdom,* London, 1975, Neville Spearman.

Crowley, A., *Book 4,* Dallas, 1972, Sangreal Foundation.

Crowley, A., *Magick in Theory and Practice,* published privately in Paris, 1929.

Crowley, A., *The Qabalah of Aleister Crowley,* New York, 1973, Samuel Weiser.

Drury, N., *The Path of the Chameleon,* London, 1973, Neville Spearman.

Drury, N. and Skinner, S., *The Search for Abraxas,* London, 1972, Neville Spearman.

Halevi, Z. S., *Adam and the Kabbalistic Tree,* London, 1974, Rider.

Heenan, E. F., *Mystery, Magic and Miracle: Religion in a Post-Aquarian Age,* Englewood Cliffs, New Jersey, 1973, Prentice-Hall.

Howe, E., *The Magicians of the Golden Dawn,* London, 1972, Routledge & Kegan Paul.

Hughes, R. *Heaven and Hell in Western Art,* London, 1968, Weidenfeld & Nicolson.

King, F. (ed.), *Astral Projection, Magic and Alchemy,* London, 1973, Neville Spearman.

King, F. (ed), *Ritual Magic in England,* London, 1970, Neville Spearman.

King, F. and Skinner, S., *Techniques of High Magic,* London, 1976, C. W. Daniel.

Mathers, S. L., *The Kabbalah Unveiled,* London, 1968, Routledge & Kegan Paul

Mathers, S. L., *The Sacred Magic of Abramelin the Mage,* Chicago, 1948, De Laurence.

Pauwels, L. and Bergier, J., *The Dawn of Magic,* London, 1963, Anthony Gibbs and Phillips — subsequently retitled *The Morning of the Magicians.*

Regardie, I., *The Golden Dawn,* Vols 1-4, Chicago, 1937-40, Aries Press.

Regardie, I., *The Tree of Life,* London, 1932, Rider.

Schaya, L., *The Universal Meaning of the Kabbalah,* 1971, New Jersey, University Books Inc.

Scholem, G., *Kabbalah,* New York, 1975, Quadrangle/New York Times.

Bibliography

Spare, A. 0. *The Book of Pleasure*, Montreal, 1976, 93 Publishing.

Waite, A. E., *The Brotherhood of the Rosy Cross*, New York, 1961, University Books

Waite, A. E., *The Holy Kabbalah*, New York, 1960, University Books Inc.

Waite, A. E., *The Pictorial Key to the Tarot*, New York, 1973, Samuel Weiser.

Watson, C., *The Occult*, London, 1971, Hodder & Stoughton.

Zaretsky, H. and Leone, M. (eds), *Religious Movements in Contemporary America*, 1974, Princeton University Press.

Zimmer, H,. *The King and the Corpse*, New York, 1960, Meridian.

Chapter 2: Archetypes and Belief Systems

Butler, W. E., *Magic, The Ritual Power and Purpose*, London, 1958, Aquarian Press.

Butler, W. E., *The Magician, his Training and Work*, London, 1959, Aquarian Press.

Edinger, E., *Ego and Archetype*, Baltimore, 1973, Penguin Books.

Eliade, M., *Cosmos and History*, New York, 1959, Harper & Row.

Eliade, M., *Shamanism*, London, 1952, Routledge & Kegan Paul.

Fortune, D., *Applied Magic*, London, 1962, Aquarian Press.

Fortune, D., *The Mystical Qabalah*, London, 1966, Ernest Benn.

Henderson, J., *The Thresholds of Initiation*, Connecticut, 1967, Wesleyan University Press.

Jacobi, J., *The Psychology of C. G. Jung*, London, 1942, Routledge & Kegan Paul.

Jung, C. G., *The Archetypes of the Collective Unconscious*, London, 1959, Routledge & Kegan Paul.

Jung, C. G., *Aion*, London, 1959, Routledge & Kegan Paul.

Jung, C. G., *Man and his Symbols*, London, 1964, Aldus Books.

Jung. C. G., *Memories, Dreams and Reflections*, London, 1967, Fontana Books.

Jung. C. G., *Modern Man in Search of a Soul*, London, 1933, Routledge & Kegan Paul.

Jung. C. G., *The Integration of the Personality*, London, 1940, Kegan Paul, Trench, Trubner.

Jung. C. G., *The Structure and Dynamics of the Psyche*, London, 1959, Routledge & Kegan Paul.

Jung. C. G., *VII Sermones ad Mortuos*, London, 1967, Stuart & Watkins.

Lilly, J., *Centre of the Cyclone*, London, 1973, Paladin.

Lilly, J., *The Dyadic Cyclone*, New York, 1976, Simon & Schuster.

Lilly, J., *The Human Biocomputer*, London, 1974, Abacus.

Lilly, J., *Simulations of God*, New York, 1975, Simon & Schuster,

Regardie, I., *The Art and Meaning of Magic*, Cheltenham, 1964, Helios.

Roszak, T., *Unfinished Animal*, New York, 1975, Harper & Row.

Wolff, F. M., *Pathways Through to Space*, New York, 1973, Julian Press.

Chapter 3: The Tarot and Transformation

Blakeley, J. D., *The Mystical Tower of the Tarot*, London, 1974, Robinson &

Watkins.

Butler, B., *The Definitive Tarot*, London, 1975, Rider.

Butler, W. E., *Magic and the Qabalah*, London, 1964, Aquarian Press.

Case, P.F., *The Tarot*, New York, 1947, Macoy.

Cavendish, R., *The Tarot*, London, 1975, Michael Joseph.

Crowley, A., *The Book of Thoth*, New York, 1969, Samuel Weiser.

Drury, N., *Don Juan, Mescalito and Modern Magic*, London and Boston, 1977, Routledge & Kegan Paul.

Drury, N. (ed.), *Frontiers of Consciousness*, Melbourne, 1975, Greenhouse Press.

Drury, N., *The Path of the Chameleon*, London, 1973, Neville Spearman.

Eliade, M., *Shamanism*, London, 1952, Routledge & Kegan Paul.

Fortune, D., *The Mystical Qabalah*, 1966, London, Ernest Benn.

Gettings, F., *The Book of the Tarot*, London, 1973, Trewin Copplestone Publishing.

Gray, W. G., *The Ladder of Lights*, Cheltenham, 1968, Hellos.

Hoellier, S. A., *The Royal Road*, Wheaton, Illinois, 1975, Quest Books.

Kaplan, S. R., *Tarot Classic*, New York, 1972, Grosset & Dunlap.

King, F. (ed.), *Astral Projection, Magic and Alchemy*, London, 1971, Neville Spearman.

Knight, G., *A Practical Guide to Qabalistic Symbolism*, Vols 1 and 2, Cheltenham, 1965, Helios.

Levi, E., *The History of Magic*, London, 1913, Rider.

Miller, D., *The New Polytheism*, New York, 1974, Harper & Row.

Ouspensky, P.D., *7he Symbolism of the Tarot*, New York, 1976, Dover.

Regardie, I., *The Golden Dawn*, Vols 1-4, Chicago, 1937-40, Aries Press.

Waite, A. E., *The Pictorial Key to the Tarot*, New York, 1963, Samuel Weiser.

Waite, A. E., *The Mysteries of Magic*, New Jersey, 1974., University Books Inc.

Zimmer, H., *The King and the Corpse*, New York, 1960, Meridian.

Chapter 4: Surrealism and the Qabalah

Balakian, A., *Surrealism: The Road to the Absolute*, London 1973, Allen and Unwin

Cardinal, R., and Short, R.S., *Surrealism: Permanent Revolution*, London 1970, Studio Vista

Diehl, G., *Max Ernst*, New York 1973, Crown

Deren, M., *Divine Horsemen: Voodoo Gods of Haiti*, London 1970, Thames & Hudson

Drury, N. and Skinner, S., *The Search for Abraxas*, London 1972, Spearman

Ernst, M., *Maximiliana*, Munich 1975, Bruckmann

Fadiman, J., and Frager,R,., *Personality and Personal Growth*. New York 1976, Harper & Row Avon

Larkin, D., *Dali*, London 1974, Pan Books

Levy, J., *Surrealism*, New York 1968, Arno

Lippard, L. (ed.) *Surrealists on Art*, Englewood Cliifs, New Jersey 1970, Prentice-Hall

Matthews, J.H., *An Introduction to Surrealism*, 1965, Pennsylvania State University Press

Bibliography

Russell, J., *Max Ernst*, London 1967, Thames & Hudson
Soby, J.T., *Magritte*, New York 1965, Museum of Modern Art
Soby, J.T. *Yves Tanguy*, New York 1955, Museum of Modern Art
Spies, W., *Max Ernst 1950-1970*, New York 1971, Abrams
Sylvester, D., *Magritte*, London 1969, Arts Council of Great Britain
Terrasse, A., *Paul Delvaux*, Chicago 1973, Philip O'Hara
Van Dusen, W., *The Natural Depth in Man*, New York 1972, Harper & Row
Waldberg, P., *Surrealism*, London 1965, Thames & Hudson
Waldo-Schwarz, P., *Art and the Occult*, New York 1975, Braziller
White, J., (ed.) *Frontiers of Consciousness*, New York 1975,
Xuriguera, G., *Wifredo Lam*, Paris 1974, Filipacchi

Chapter 5: *The Magic of Austin Spare*
Beskin, G., and Bonner, J., *Austin Osman Spare 1886-1956 - The Divine Draughtsman*, London 1987, Beskin Press
Drury, N., and Skinner, S., *The Search for Abraxas*, London 1972, Spearman
Grant, K., *Images and Oracles of Austin Osman Spare*, London 1975, Muller
Grant, K., 'Austin Osman Spare', *Hidden Lore*, London 1989, Skoob Books
Spare, A., *Earth Inferno*, London 1905, privately printed
Spare, A., *A Book of Satyrs*, London 1907, privately printed
Spare, A., *A Book of Pleasure (Self-Love); The Psychology of Ecstasy*, London 1913 (republished by 93 Publishing, Montreal 1975)
Spare, A., *The Focus of Life*, London 1976, Askin
Spare, A., *The Anathema of Zos: the Sermon to the Hypocrites*, reprinted London 1973, *Agape* Vol.1 No.4
Spare, A., *A Book of Automatic Drawings*, London 1972, Catalpa Press

Chapter 6: *The Supernatural World of Rosaleen Norton*
Drury, N. and Tillett, G., *Other Temples, Other Gods*, Sydney 1980, Methuen
Drury,N., *Pan's Daughter: The Magical World of Rosaleen Norton*, Oxford 1993, Mandrake
Norton, R., and Greenlees,G., *The Art of Rosaleen Norton*, Sydney 1982 (facsimile edition), Walter Glover
Norton, R., *Supplement to The Art of Rosaleen Norton*, Sydney 1984, Walter Glover

Chapter 7: *Beyond the New Age*
Adler, M., *Drawing Down the Moon*, Boston 1988, Beacon Press
Bolen, J.S., *Goddesses in Everywoman*, New York 1985, Harper & Row
Campbell, J., *The Hero with a Thousand Faces*, New Jersey 1948, Princeton University Press
Drury, N., *The Elements of Human Potential*, Dorset 1989, Element
Drury, N., (ed.) *The Bodywork Book*, Dorset 1984, Prism
Drury, N., (ed.) *Inner Health*, Dorset 1985, Prism
Grof, S., *The Adventure of Self-Discovery*, Albany 1985, State University of

New York Press

Harner, M., *The Way of the Shaman*, San Francisco 1990, Harper Collins

Houston, J., 'Myth and Pathos in Sacred Psychology', *Dromenon*, Vol. 3 No.2., Spring 1981

Houston, J., *The Possible Human*, Los Angeles 1982, Tarcher

Houston, J., *The Search for the Beloved*, Los Angeles, 1987, Tarcher

Knaster, M., 'The Goddesses in Jean Shinoda Bolen', *East West*, March 1989

Millikan,D., and Drury, N., *Worlds Apart: Christianity and the New Age*, Sydney 1991, Australian Broadcasting Corporation

Starhawk, *The Spiral Dance*, San Francisco 1979, Harper & Row

Starhawk, *Dreaming the Dark*, Boston 1982, Beacon Press

Tart, C., (ed.) *Transpersonal Psychologies*, New York 1975, Harper & Row

Williams, V., 'The Sacred Craft', *East West*, October 1984

Chapter 8: Contemporary Shamanism and the Earth Mother

Albert,M., 'Out of Africa', *Yoga Journal*, January/February 1985

Boyer, R., 'The Vision Quest', *The Laughing Man*, Vol,2 No.4

Halifax, J., *Shamanic Voices*, New York 1979, Dutton

Jamal,M., *Shape Shifters*, London 1987, Arkana

Harner, M., *The Way of the Shaman*, San Francisco 1990, HarperCollins

Kalweit,H., *Dreamtime and Inner Space*, Boston 1988, Shambhala

Neubert,R., 'Sun Bear: Walking in Balance on the Earth Mother', *New Realities*, May/June 1987

Nicholson, S. (ed.), *Shamanism*, Wheaton 1987, Quest Books

Sun Bear and Wabun *The Medicine Wheel*, Englewood Cliffs 1980, Prentice-Hall

Teish,L., *Jambalaya*, San Francisco 1985, Harper & Row

Chapter 9: Sacred Plants and Mystic Realities

McKenna, D., and McKenna, T., *The Invisible Landscape*, New York 1975, Seabury Press

McKenna, T.,*The Archaic Revival*, San Francisco 1991, HarperCollins

McKenna,T,. *True Hallucinations*, San Francisco 1993, HarperCollins

Abraham, R., McKenna,T., and Sheldrake,R., *Trialogues at the Edge of the West*, Santa Fe 1992, Bear & Co.

Chapter 10: Computers, Consciousness and Creativity

Leary, T., *Flashbacks: An Autobiography*, Los Angeles 1983, Tarcher

Leary, T., *High Priest*, New York 1968, College Notes & Texts/New American Library

Stevens, J., *Storming Heaven: LSD and the American Dream*, New York 1987, Atlantic Monthly Press

INDEX